ERA MAN

Historic racing with W.R.G. (Bill) Morris

ERA MAN

Historic racing with W.R.G. (Bill) Morris

by

Tim May

Morris Publications

© text 2011 Tim May
© photos 2011 individual photographers

First published 2011 by Morris Publications,
Lower Ashmead House, 56 Lower End, Leafield, Oxfordshire OX29 9QJ
Further copies may be obtained from David Kergon, 10/12 Alpe St, Ipswich, IP1 3NZ
or by email to: david.kergon@btinternet.com

ISBN 0-9544340-0-5

All rights reserved. No part of this publication may be reproduced, stored in a retrieval system, or transmitted, in any form or by any means, electronic, mechanical, photocopying, recording or otherwise, without the prior permission of the authors.

The reproduction of any part of the text or any of the illustrations in whole or in part is forbidden without written permission from the copyright holders.

Designed and produced by Charlie Webster, Minster Lovell
Printed in Great Britain by Information Press, Eynsham, Oxford

Contents

Foreword *by Victoria Morris*   7

Introduction *by Tim May*   9

Acknowledgements   11

Chapter One
R12B and R12C – the years before 1962   13

Chapter Two
Enter Bill Morris and David Kergon – the first years with Hanuman II   29

Chapter Three
Bill and Hanuman II – from the 1970s to the 1990s   55

Chapter Four
R12C recreated – from the 1960s to the 1990s   84

Chapter Five
Reviving and racing Romulus   111

Chapter Six
Racing an E type, 1989-1993   133

Chapter Seven
ERA man in and out of the workshop   145

Footnote   163

Index   165

Bill in R12C at Oulton Park in June 1998

Foreword

This book was originally commissioned by my husband William (Bill) Morris in order to record the history of his ERAs R12B and R12C, and to explain why the two ERAs shared the same chassis number and the name Hanuman. He also wished to record his lifetime involvement in historic racing which, viewed from today's perspective, covered a particularly rich era of the sport.

The book has been written by Tim May, who, with his longstanding involvement with the ERA Club, was Bill's obvious choice. The two collaborated together until Bill's untimely death in 2009. A welcome contributor was David Kergon, Bill's original co-owner of the two cars; another was Tony Stephens with regard to his involvement with ERA R12C.

By the time he died, the book's remit had widened to include Bill's experiences with another two ERAs; R2B Romulus and the E type ERA GP2.

Many people, too numerous to mention, have contributed memories and material to help make this book a fitting tribute to Bill and his ERAs, along with the historic racing scene he enjoyed so much. I hope it reminds us all of his vitality, integrity and good-humoured enthusiasm for these amazing racing cars.

My grateful thanks to you all for helping me finish this book for Bill and Tim.

Victoria Morris
Leafield, 2011

Tim May is standing by R12B Hanuman II at Oulton Park in August 2002. Tim's wife, Gillian, is on the left and their eldest son, Nick, and eldest grandson, Joseph, are in the driver's seat.

Introduction

Bill Morris' original invitation to write an account of his two ERAs was a surprise – though a very pleasant one. Although I grew up in a strong motor sport family, my own involvement in ERA has been strictly as a 'camp follower'. I saw ERAs at an impressionable age and as the other boys admired Spitfires or Jubilee class railway engines I latched on to ERA. Their activities have remained a life-long interest and from the early 1980s the ERA Club has provided a continuing opportunity to record and write about them.

The book begins with a 'pre-Bill' chapter outlining R12B's creation and racing activities before Bill and David Kergon bought it in 1962. It unravels the origins of R12B and R12C to make clear why and how two ERAs derived from what was originally a single car. Chapters Two and Three focus on R12B Hanuman II – Chapter Two describing Bill and David's first steps and the following chapter focusing on how things changed in later decades. Chapter Four concentrates on the recreation of R12C in the 1960s and 1970s and Bill's subsequent major rebuild in the 1990s. Chapters Five and Six are about the other two ERAs which Bill worked on and raced – R2B Romulus and the E type GP2. Finally Chapter Seven deals with a number of other aspects of Bill's ERA life – as the 'gearbox man', as writer and correspondent and as someone who provided an important source of encouragement to other drivers and engineers.

Many people have contributed to the account that follows and I'm extremely grateful for their co-operation. Two whom I would like to single out here are Bill and Victoria Morris. Bill gave me the opportunity to write about his ERA experience in the first place and, in addition to much documentation, responded very fully to any queries I raised. Victoria Morris has been a keen supporter of this project from its inception and after Bill's death has devoted much time, energy and organisational skill to bringing it to final fruition.

Tim May

Acknowledgements

Grateful thanks are due to the following for permission to use their photos. We regret any accidental omissions.

Stuart Bennett	Jim McDonald
Pam Bramwell	Ben Morris
Terence Brettell	Victoria Morris
Neil Bruce	The NZ Herald/Wilson & Norton Ltd
James Brymer	Otago Daily Press/Allied Press Ltd
Narisa Chakrabongse	Roger Richmond
Alan Cox	Pierre Roggero
Franco Fiumefreddo	E Selwyn-Smith
Ground Sky Photography	Glenda Snape
David Kergon	June Spollon
Geoffrey Kergon	Len Thorpe
LAT Photographic	The VSCC
Tim May	Michael Ware
Oliver McCrossan	David Weguelin

Chapter One

R12B and R12C – the years before 1962

This chapter tells the story of R12B/R12C from its origins in 1936 until it was bought by Bill and David Kergon in 1962. Bill spent his whole racing life with historic racing cars and a vital element with the great majority of such cars is their continuous competition history, often stretching over many decades. More especially the ERA that first emerged in 1936 as R12B underwent quite a complicated historical journey. To understand how and why there came to be two very closely related ERAs, R12B and R12C, the story needs to be followed through from the beginning.

ERA: origins and design

The story of the ERA Company and the cars it created is a fairly familiar one so its main features need only a brief recital. The Company was founded in the autumn of 1933 to build voiturette racing cars. The three key individuals were Raymond Mays, Peter Berthon and Humphrey Cook. Mays and Berthon had run a car known as The White Riley in 1933 which incorporated various modifications to a standard Riley sports design. Peter Berthon had improved the engine and Tom Murray Jamieson had supplied a supercharger. Humphrey Cook thought the car had distinct possibilities if it underwent further development and offered to put up the necessary capital so that a limited programme of manufacture could be undertaken.

A small factory was established in Raymond Mays' lifetime home at Bourne in Lincolnshire and the first car emerged from there in May 1934. Initially the A type car was produced, of which there were four; it was succeeded by the B type which incorporated small changes and thirteen chassis were laid down. R12B which is one of the central characters in this story was the penultimate B type chassis.

Important elements of the White Riley, particularly its engine and supercharger, became part of the ERA's specification. The Riley six-cylinder engine, which had been the basis for Berthon's development, incorporated two valves for each of its cylinders, with two camshafts set

R12B only had a brief life as a B type ERA. Here Mays is making FTD at the very wet Shelsley Meeting in September 1936. R12B was fitted with a two-litre Zoller-blown engine.

high on each side of the block operating via push rods and rockers. The standard bore and stroke was 57 x 95.5 (1488 cc) but 1100cc and two litre versions were also used. The chassis, designed by Reid Railton, expressed the orthodoxy of the period with semi-elliptic springs, friction shock absorbers and rod-operated brakes. One feature that was not common on competition cars at the time was the use of a pre-selector gearbox. Unlike the White Riley, which was ostensibly a two-seater, the ERA had a proper single-seater body with the seat set high to clear the torque tube.

The beginning of R12B

R12B only existed in its original form for a few months. Although in the pre-war years chassis numbers were not always recorded, it seems very likely that its debut was at the June 1936 Shelsley Walsh hill climb as a works-entered two–litre car driven by Raymond Mays. However, as it failed in practice, its real debut was at the second Shelsley meeting of 1936 held in September where in very wet conditions it set FTD. Mays registered another success with the car when he won the Mountain Championship at Brooklands in October. And that was the end of the first phase of the car's history as it was converted to C type specification in the winter of 1936/7.

Conversion: R12B becomes R12C

R12B had been fitted with a Zoller supercharger when it competed at Shelsley and Brooklands. The works cars began experimenting with the Zoller unit in 1935 and continued to do so throughout 1936. Its great attraction was the power boost it provided compared to the standard Murray Jamieson unit, but this improvement was far from cost free. There were two main problems – first the complexities of the Zoller and second its impact on the rest of the ERA design. The Zoller lacked the reliability of the Jamieson blower and imposed a heavy charge on the resources – always stretched – of the ERA Company. It led to difficulties between the three key personnel in the Company – Mays, Berthon and Cook. The first two were strongly committed to the Zoller and its problems in no way altered their conviction that it was the right way to go. Cook, on the other hand, was highly sceptical given the Zoller's unreliability and the poor results it had led to during 1936.

However, on this occasion, Mays and Berthon won the argument. Not only did they succeed in persuading Cook that the Zoller should be used, but they were also able to convince him that modifications should be made to some of the basic features of the A and B type cars. These changes acknowledged that the Zoller's power boost strained some aspects of the original ERA design. The 1937 works C type ERAs incorporated various features designed to deal with these problems. The most important changes were the adoption of a Porsche-designed i.f.s. together with adjustments to the springs and shock absorbers; hydraulic actuation for the brakes; and stronger connecting rods and alterations to the bearings and crankshaft. The external appearance of the C types was also slightly modified due to the i.f.s. and a larger fuel tank.

It's worth emphasising that the two works C types, R4C and R12C, did not have entirely new chassis. What happened was that the front half of the existing B type chassis was sawn off and a new boxed section welded on to which the i.f.s. was attached. The Porsche i.f.s. was very expensive and it was clear that repairing or replacing it would be a major undertaking. As we shall see, this proved to be the case with R12C in 1939.

R12C 1937–1939: success, and then an undoing

After its brief period as R12B, the conversion to R12C produced a car that had an overwhelmingly successful record, initially as a works car in 1937 and then with the Chula/Bira équipe in 1938-9. This successful period culminated in a serious accident which had major consequences for the car's future.

As a works car R12C's main drivers were Pat Fairfield and Arthur Dobson; occasionally Raymond Mays and Humphrey Cook also had a drive. Although there were teething problems with the new hydraulically-operated brakes other elements of the C type 'package' gelled together successfully. In particular the Zoller superchargers on both

R12B was converted to R12C in the winter of 1936/7. These two photos show some of its key features.

The White Mouse photo (top) shows R12C's engine with the rear-mounted Zoller supercharger above the gearbox.

Pat Fairfield winning the Coronation Cup at Crystal Palace in May 1937. The distinctive Porsche i.f.s. can be seen; unusually R12C is running on 16-inch front wheels rather than 18-inch. Peter Berthon had decided to fit the smaller wheels to overcome problems with the brakes.

R4C and R12C proved far more reliable than in 1936 though at the cost of absorbing a disproportionate amount of preparation time.

Given R12C's good record in 1937 it would not have been surprising if the works had kept it for 1938 along with its stablemate, R4C. However it was only the latter car they retained, using it as a basis for a further transformation, as R4C gave way to R4D. One reason for disposing of R12C was that the Chula/Bira équipe (often known as the White Mouse team) wanted to add a C type ERA to their stable. In 1937 the Siamese team's plans had unravelled badly. They had bought the Delage raced with great success during 1936 by Dick Seaman and then attempted to modify it, chiefly by commissioning a new chassis with i.f.s. Unfortunately this Delage project never bore fruit although it cost a great deal of money and led to the resignation of their chief mechanic in mid-1937. Having seen the works C types in action during 1937 they concluded that if the Delage

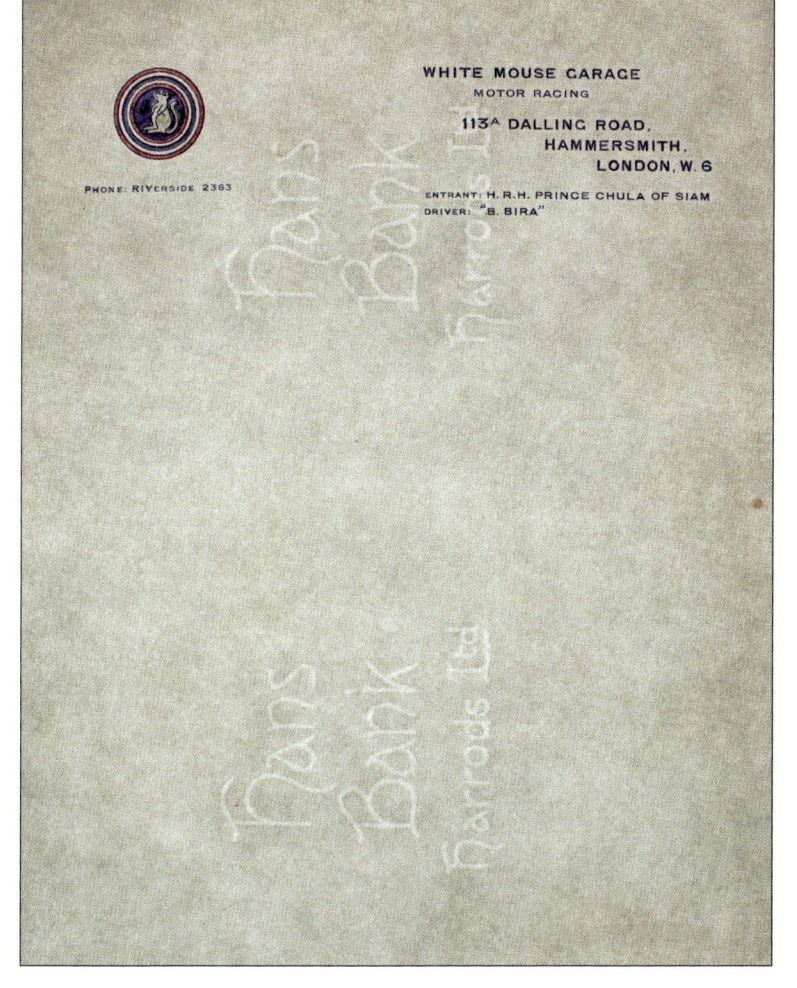

The notepaper used by Chula and Bira. Held up to the light, the paper reveals a Harrods watermark: only the best was good enough for the White Mouse team. Chula and Bira adopted a small white mouse symbol in 1935 when they began racing. Chula's Siamese nickname was 'nou' which translates as 'mouse'.

Bira winning the Cork Light Car Race in April 1938. R12C has been re-sprayed a light blue and is now on 18-inch front wheels. It has been overhauled by 'Lofty' England after its purchase from the works and Bira has named it Hanuman.

wouldn't work they could only remain competitive by acquiring a C type. Accordingly a deal was done and R12C left Bourne and moved to Dalling Road, Hammersmith in West London, where the White Mouse team had their headquarters.

R12C was rebuilt by Lofty England and repainted in Bira blue for the start of the 1938 season. The colour scheme was changed again in 1939 when Siam became a member of the A.I.A.C.R. and was entitled to its own national racing colours. Blue and yellow were chosen: blue preserved the existing colour and it was combined with yellow which was the colour of the Siamese Royal Family. Yellow was used for the chassis and wheels, blue for the remainder. It was a striking combination which always made the car very easy to distinguish.

Apart from the new coat of paint the only other difference in R12C's appearance was the substitution of the oblong driving mirrors for round ones and its identification as Hanuman. When the White Mouse stable's original ERA (R2B) was joined by an identical car (R5B) in 1936 Bira chose the names Romulus and Remus to differentiate them. R12C's name was taken from the Sanskrit epic poem, the Ramayana: "Hanuman was a demi-god in the shape of a white monkey who could perform great feats of skill and daring and was the most beloved figure of all" (Chula: *Road Star Hat Trick*, p.122). The name was displayed in small letters on each side of the scuttle together with a silver badge depicting the monkey god.

In the two seasons, 1938 and 1939 Bira drove R12C – or Hanuman as we should now call it – in ten events altogether – eight in 1938 and two in 1939. He continued the successful record that had been established in

Bira in R12C in the assembly area at Donington prior to the start of the 1939 Nuffield Trophy. R12C is now is a blue and yellow colour scheme; the white mouse symbol can be seen on the scuttle and a Hanuman badge on the bonnet.

This photo shows the Porsche-designed independent front suspension which had the 'long arms'. When the reconstruction of R12C was begun in the 1960s no spare long arm i.f.s parts were available so R12C was fitted with a spare short arm set originally made for R4D.

Bira at Reims, July 1939, just prior to the accident.

1937 with only a few hiccups until the accident in July 1939. Among Bira's scalps were two victories in the Nuffield Trophy, as well as wins at Brooklands and in Ireland.

However for our tale of R12B and R12C in the Bill Morris years, it was the accident at Reims which had the most significant long-term impact. While the broad details of the accident are fairly well known, its consequences have not always been accurately described.

Bira's accident occurred during practice for the 1500cc race which was a curtain-raiser for the French G.P. of 1939. Arthur Dobson driving the works E type ERA had set a slightly better practice time than Bira. Bira and Hanuman were sent out for a final lap or two to check fuel consumption. But Bira didn't have only fuel consumption in mind: "What if I were to put up the fastest time of the day this coming lap, would the green works ERA have to go out again, and wouldn't that worry the life out of the team" (Bira: *Bits and Pieces*, p. 13)

Unfortunately it all went wrong. He took a left hand bend too fast, a skid ensued and one of the wheels dug into sandy soil on the edge of the track. Bira tried to regain control but failed as the car shot backwards until it hit a soft sandbank very hard. The impact threw the car into the air ejecting Bira who, most fortunately, had a soft landing in some bushes. The car then rolled over a number of times before coming to rest. Chula summed up the result: "The car was severely damaged. The fuel tank was smashed with fuel flowing out freely, so it was lucky the car did not catch fire and prove a total loss. The bodywork was well bashed in, the radiator broken and some parts of the expensive independent suspension were damaged" (Chula: *Blue and Yellow*, p.70)

Two pictures taken at Reims in the wake of the crash indicating the general impact of the accident on R12C.

R12C is back in the White Mouse Garage with the damage evident from the crash at Reims.

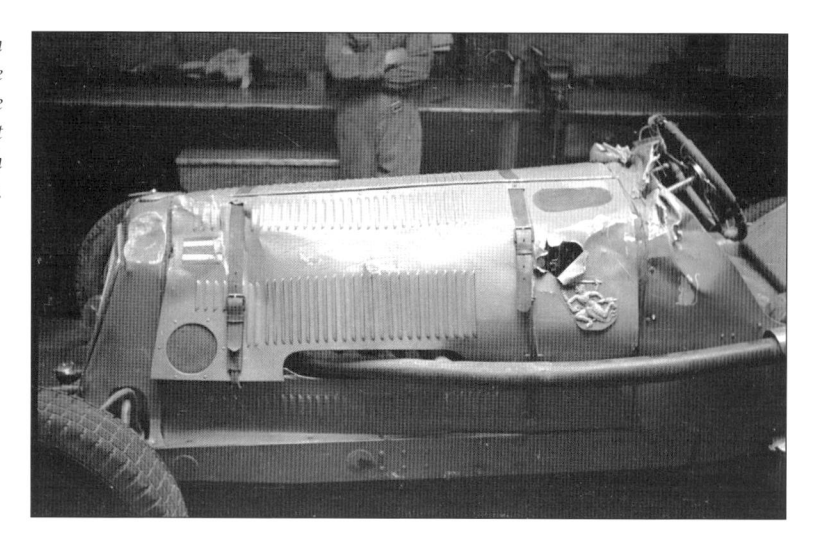

Reconstruction: back to R12B?

As Chula's words indicate, if there had been a fire it's highly likely that R12C would have been the second ERA to disappear for ever – that sad fate having befallen R3B after Marcel Lehoux's fatal accident in 1936. Happily, that was not the outcome, but the reconstruction faced some major problems. Some important components could be used in the rebuild – the engine and supercharger, the gearbox and the back axle. Even the chassis was not beyond repair, some descriptions of it as 'mangled' or 'twisted' exaggerate its problems and, as we shall see, it was successfully repaired many years later.

The silver Thai Hanuman badge was removed and mounted onto the steering wheel after the accident, and kept as a memento by Prince Chula.

The key problem was not the chassis but the i.f.s. This had been badly damaged, especially on one side. Stanley Holgate, the White Mouse team's chief mechanic did endeavour to get it repaired. Bill Morris' understanding is that the suspension was sent to Laystalls for repair, but as luck would have it their works suffered bomb damage and so that possibility was, literally, extinguished. On this interpretation the rebuilding of the car took place gradually during the war; David Weguelin, author of the famous book *The History of English Racing Automobiles Limited*, doesn't mention Laystalls, however, and says the whole car was reconstructed by November 1939.

Whichever time-scale is correct, there is no dispute that the i.f.s. could not be repaired or re-used and it therefore followed that the C type chassis could not serve as the basis of the reconstruction. That meant substituting an A or B type chassis and although ERA didn't produce spare chassis one was available as a by-product of the C and D type rebuilds.

The chassis that was used had previously been on Earl Howe's car, R8B. Howe's car was the third ERA to be converted from B to C type specification. If it had followed the precedent of R4B and R12B the conversion would have utilised some of the existing chassis and thus there would have been no spare for the White Mouse team. Most fortuitously Howe's conversion took place a year later, in 1937-8 and at the same time the works were converting R4C into R4D. Crucially the D type conversion used a brand new chassis always distinguishable by the drilled holes along both chassis rails. Therefore R4C's chassis was available to convert Howe's car into a C type, freeing up R8B's chassis for Hanuman's reconstruction.

The complete car was therefore a mixture of B and C type elements: a B type chassis with conventional semi-elliptic front suspension but a C type engine with a Zoller supercharger and hydraulic brakes. Identity games could now be played – should the car continue to be known as R12C or was R12B/C more accurate or even R8B since it was built on that car's chassis frame. Chula recognised it was a distinct entity saying that the Reims crash meant that the original Hanuman "virtually ceased to exist" and the rebuilt car should be known as Hanuman II. He said the same thing again many years later when Bill Morris and David Kergon were just re-introducing the car to British racing, but before we reach that point a little more needs to be said about its post-war racing history.

Bira on his way to victory in the 1946 Ulster Trophy race. R12C has now been rebuilt on a B type chassis and is known as R12B Hanuman II from now on. The B type solid axle has De Ram dampers mounted in a distinctive way.

Post-War history: 1946-1962

As soon as motor racing resumed the Chula/Bira partnership returned to the circuits and Hanuman II was entered for the 1946 Ulster Trophy which Bira won. There were three more events in 1947 for Hanuman II, but none of these outings were successful and during 1948 Chula decided he didn't want to continue motor racing.

Hanuman II was raced during 1949/50 by David Hampshire and David Murray with Hampshire doing nearly all the long-distance races; David Murray had a single (but successful) circuit event with the car and a couple of class wins in Scottish hill climbs. Murray and Hampshire were part of the Reg Parnell/Ashmore brothers' équipe and the precise ownership of R12B isn't completely clear – when the car next changed hands the cheque was made out to Parnell but he may have been the agent for Murray and Hampshire rather than the owner.

By the time Hampshire and Murray bought the car the position of ERAs was changing. In the immediate post-war years they were eligible for grand prix races and as there were few other single-seater cars they were sought after and commanded a high price. But by 1949/50 the supply of racing cars had increased and ERAs were less favoured. Furthermore the formula that qualified them as grand prix cars was due to end in 1951. Of course they had been designed for voiturette racing not grand prix work and because their basic design dated back to the early 1930s, there was a strong imperative while they were in front-line

R12B Hanuman II seen with three subsequent owners after leaving the White Mouse stable.

David Hampshire is shown winning his class in the 1949 speed trials along the promenade at Weston-Super-Mare. Note that the De Rams have now been replaced with lever hydraulic dampers with a connecting bar between steel side plates.

Jim Somervail at Goodwood in June 1954 at the Whitsun Trophy road race.

racing to keep them as competitive as possible. Many owners responded by altering things like superchargers, springs and shock absorbers, axle damping and bodywork. Hanuman II felt the impact of some of these changes with the removal of its Zoller supercharger and modifications to its springs and shock absorbers.

Dropping the Zoller supercharger might seem contradictory, effectively giving up a more powerful blower for a less powerful one. It was a decision dictated chiefly by the need for reliability, which was important in qualifying for the much needed starting money. Although the Zoller supercharger had worked well in 1937-9 its maintenance costs were high and the more constrained post-war climate made it too risky. Substituting a Jamieson supercharger for the Zoller meant re-mixing the B and C type elements in Hanuman II and its chassis number was now usually quoted as R12B. Two other changes made to many ERAs, ZF differentials and rear radius rods didn't feature on Hanuman II during this period. In fact it was never fitted with radius rods but did finally acquire a ZF differential in the early 1980s.

When Hampshire and Murray moved on to more modern cars, Hanuman II was sold to a Scottish Borders farmer, Jim Somervail. Jim was a member of Border Reivers, a collection of Scottish drivers who combined together for mutual support. In the early 1950s when Jim was driving Hanuman II, ERAs continued to move away from the spotlight to a more marginal position. This change was reflected in the price at which they changed hands, a few hundred pounds usually sufficing and the rapid rate at which they moved from one owner to the next. ERAs were not only more marginal but more fragmented in their competition activity – a few, including Hanuman II, lingered in Formula Libre events, some concentrated on hill climbs and sprints, a small number began to compete in historic events, and some were entirely inactive.

Somervail concentrated on racing at Scottish ex-airfield circuits such as Charterhall, Turnberry and Winfield, though he did occasionally make the long journey down to Goodwood. He didn't know a great deal about ERAs prior to acquiring Hanuman II and he didn't have much contact with other ERA owners and drivers. It was very much a case of learning by experience and he was always concerned about the risk of damaging the car both mechanically and through off-course excursions. Jim says that compared to Ecurie Ecosse, the other well-known Scottish racing team who "always had lots of money", Border Reivers "were nearly always broke" and when things went wrong the imperative was to repair rather than replace. When a Cooper Bristol came into the Border Reivers team Jim found it a more straightforward proposition both to drive and to maintain and it was time for Hanuman II to move on again.

In fact its British racing career came to a temporary end in 1954 and nine years were to pass before it appeared in a UK event again. Initially it was sold to Denys Owen who intended to use it for VSCC events, but due to insurance and family problems never raced it. He passed it on in turn to Ken Flint and Verdun Edwards at Autospeed Garage in Liverpool. They had various sporting cars through their hands in the 1950s including three ERAs, R5B *(Remus)* and the two E types, GP1 and GP2.

Ken and Verdun never raced Hanuman II; it's most likely that they bought it always intending to sell it on. Their buyer was Sam Tingle living in what was then Southern Rhodesia and since 1980 Zimbabwe. Sam was familiar with ERAs having seen R3A racing in South Africa as

The car when it was owned by Denys Owen. It has been towed out to a deserted country lane to be started-up and driven around the countryside! During Somervail's ownership Hanuman II was repainted dark blue.

R12B in South Africa – probably with Sam Tingle at the wheel, The car is in the same colour scheme as its Border Reivers days, except for the wheels which are now painted silver.

R12B Hanuman ll in Salisbury, Southern Rhodesia in July 1962; this is certainly the final event in Africa before it came back to the UK. Note the local opposition! The very large lever hydraulic shock absorbers can be seen in the photograph above. It has now reverted to a yellow chassis and blue body work, but the wheels are still silver.

well as a more recent 'import', the ex-Bob Gerard R4A. A friend who was travelling to the U.K. was asked to inspect Hanuman II at Autospeed and on the basis of his report Sam agreed to pay £450 for it.

Sam Tingle had had a fair amount of racing experience with various MGs but when he bought Hanuman II he didn't know much about the car's history or its mechanics. Echoing Jim Somervail, Sam said "It was all just get up and go in those days". When he began to drive it he found both the gearbox and the steering needed attention. Before he got down to the basic rebuild he thought it really needed – and deserved – another attractive racing car came along, one of the A type Connaughts. Sam said "I could hardly afford one racing car let alone two" so he traded the ERA against a "much-used Ford Zephyr" belonging to Alan Gillespie.

During Gillespie's ownership a friend, Vic Drummond, helped with preparation and on some occasions also drove the car. The dark blue paint it had acquired during Somervail's ownership was discarded and the Chula/Bira blue and yellow restored complete with a large lion (rampant!) on the scuttle. Drummond and Gillespie had some good outings with the car but by the early 1960s Gillespie, like Tingle before him, felt the pull of something more modern so he advertised the car in the April 1962 issue of *Motor Sport*.

Chapter Two

Enter Bill Morris and David Kergon – the first years with Hanuman II

In the beginning

Two young apprentices at Smiths Industries were enjoying a curry in Kilburn on the first Sunday in April 1962. Bill Morris and David Kergon had each bought a copy of *Motor Sport* and found, among the small ads, that Hanuman II was for sale. They quickly decided they wanted the car and negotiations were immediately set in hand.

Why was the car so attractive to them? Both had encountered ERAs as schoolboys and were much impressed. Bill said that he first saw an ERA when he was twelve and it's more or less certain this was at an Aston Martin Owner's Club meeting at Snetterton in April 1954. Three ERAs were competing in a special race for points towards a trophy donated by Humphrey Cook to mark ERA's twentieth anniversary. Raymond Mays was present and brought the flag down at the beginning and end of the race.

A subsequent visit to Snetterton in pursuit of watching ERAs had a less happy outcome for Bill, especially for his education. He was a pupil at Gresham's, the well-known school in Holt, Norfolk. With a chum Bill

This is Bill's first car, purchased for £5, complete with robin's nest in the dash board and towed home by his mother. The Austin Seven was rebuilt by Bill; bits were smuggled in to be surreptitiously worked on in the school workshops, in his boarding house trunk. Both photos were taken at Gresham's. Bill's sister, Victoria, is in the passenger seat.

The notable sheen on the tail is due to multiple applications of red paint! The 'L' plates indicate Victoria was teaching Bill to drive. He failed his driving test on his seventeenth birthday, after executing a hand signal and a racing gear change at the same time!

had gone off to another Snetterton meeting on his illegally owned 1929 Scott motorcycle. Anxious to see Bill Moss in R5B, who was running in a race at the end of the programme, Bill and his friend were forced to tear back to Holt to ensure they didn't miss chapel. Unfortunately there was a coming-together with a taxi at a cross roads: the driver, recognising their Gresham's school blazers, bundled them into his taxi and drove straight to the headmaster's study. Expulsion duly followed and Bill's father was not amused!

Bill's first mechanical explorations were into an old horizontal petrol engine found lying on a farm and bought for thirty shillings. It was stripped and re-assembled and Bill designed some belts and pulleys so that the engine could drive a small cart. However as Geoff Goddard, who along with his brother David was a 'shareholder' in the engine, remarked: "Fortunately for the work load of the local casualty hospital the design never left the drawing board!" Subsequently Geoff Goddard helped Bill strip an Austin Seven which came from the local scrap yard. Geoff thought the strip-down and rebuild was "an amazing feat because our tools were limited to a couple of hammers, a hatchet, some spanners and the odd screwdriver or two". After the rebuild, the car was used by Bill's sister; it had been painted red and as Goddard emphasised "when I say painted I mean painted. Bill had bought five gallons of surplus red paint and he was determined not to waste a drop".

Bill learnt to drive in David Goddard's Frazer-Nash and by the time he started his apprenticeship at Smiths Industries he was running a Riley which created a common bond with David Kergon who was

Bill in his Riley Special, at a garage in Porton, Wiltshire where his parents were living at the time. Gurston Down Sprint was nearby and the garage had developed a Special designed to compete at Gurston. Bill had some involvement with this Special described by David Kergon as "dangerously quick, but unstable".

Perhaps not what Smiths had in mind for student apprentices in terms of practical training! (Note they are wearing their apprentice workshop coats)!

Silverstone paddock on Friday afternoon when it was necessary ... again ... to remove the engine to re-fix the flywheel. Bill subsequently solved the problem with a little help from the tool room in Cricklewood!

These photographs were sent by Alan Gillespie to Bill Morris and David Kergon during negotiations for R12B and instigated a rapid visit by Bill's sister, Victoria, who fortunately happened to be in Salisbury at the time, to confirm that a strange engine was about to be fitted by Alan Gillespie (to make it more competitive). They advised Alan that they were only interested in purchasing the ERA if the car retained all its correct components. No mention was ever made as to the nature of the spares and these small photographs confirmed only that R12C (as indicated on the plate on the scuttle) seemed to be complete. This chassis identification plate was presumably transferred when Stan Holgate re-built the ERA during the war. Alan was really interested in obtaining a more competitive racing car and an exchange for a Lotus 18 was eventually concluded.

similarly mounted. David had been alerted to the attractions of ERAs by being taken to Shelsley in the late 1940s and early 1950s by a prep school-friend's father, where he had seen people such as Raymond Mays, Ken Wharton and Joe Fry.

Buying R12B Hanuman II

The process of buying R12B Hanuman II was not straightforward. There were two basic problems: firstly Bill and David were buying a car in a country thousands of miles away, and secondly Allan Gillespie didn't want a straightforward cheque for R12B Hanuman II. Rather fortunately, Bill's sister was in Rhodesia and she was asked to travel from Salisbury to Bulawayo to examine the car. She found it partially dismantled and after verifying the chassis details reported back. David has an idea that Gillespie was contemplating installing a Jaguar or Chevrolet engine in the car (as had been done with R4A) but this is not certain. Bill and David decided to go ahead with the purchase, subject to Gillespie putting the car back together.

For his part, although Gillespie was perfectly happy for Bill and David to have the car, he was really only interested in striking a deal which would give him a more up-to-date racing car in exchange for the ERA. It was eventually agreed that the modern car would be a Lotus 18 fitted with a Martin Ford 997cc engine. There is an amusing story surrounding this particular choice. The Lotus was bought from Mike Bond whose initial acquaintance Bill had made in less than ideal circumstances. Bond was clerk of the course at an AMOC Silverstone meeting and had been mightily displeased by Bill's driving of his Riley. After the racing Bill was duly summoned before Bond and his backside was 'thoroughly reamered' (metaphorically speaking). However calm followed the storm and Bill subsequently established quite friendly relations with Bond who suggested Bill buy him a drink after the meeting. Such relations were considerably lubricated by the alcohol (drinkable variety) in the course of which Bill disclosed that he and David had agreed to buy an ERA, subject to finding a suitable exchange. After getting over the shock at the prospect, Bond offered the Lotus and after an uninteresting testing session at Silverstone (they thought it was under-powered and wouldn't slide in the corners) it was sent to the docks for shipment to Africa.

Mike Bond had not only provided a suitable car but was helpful on the matter of the price for the Lotus. He also indicated that he wasn't

The advertisement in April 1962 Motor Sport *that began Bill and David's involvement with ERA R12B. Among the "very large collection of spares" was R12C's chassis.*

> Neale, Home Farm, Hadzor, Droitwich. Tel.: 3246. [4928
> **1940 ROLLS-ROYCE** Wraith semi-razor sports saloon. Complete engine overhaul 3,000 miles ago. History. M.O.T. certificate. Tyres good. £400. Dr. Harrowes, 8, Learmonth Terrace, Edinburgh. [4929
> **E.R.A. R12B** in Bira's racing colours of blue and yellow. Recent overhaul. A very large collection of valuable spares is included. £775 delivered to Southampton. Import duty does not apply. Further details from Murray, 120, Leicester Road, Loughborough, Tel.: 4060, or the owner, Mr. A. Gillespie, P.O. Box 1601, Salisbury, Southern Rhodesia. [4930
> **M.G.-A ROADSTER, 1958.** Blue. Hard- and soft-tops. Tonneau, luggage rack, heater, w/washers,

concerned about immediate payment provided that he *did* get paid eventually. Bond's price of £600 meant that Bill and David 'technically' made a profit as the final agreed cost of the ERA was £750. Nevertheless for two apprentices accustomed to buying and selling cars in the £100-£200 range Hanuman II's purchase price represented a hefty outlay and Bill's sister Victoria, who had checked out the car in Rhodesia, came forward with a much-appreciated loan of £100.

David and Bill had some continuing involvement with the Lotus as they subsequently sent Gillespie some Ford parts for the engine. As part payment and part wedding gift to David, Gillespie sent an animal skin to the U.K., which was smuggled in under the spare wheel of a Ford GT40. David was never quite sure which animal the skin had come from: it was probably not tiger, he thinks, but possibly cheetah or leopard; at any rate it survives with him into the twenty-first century. The owner of the GT40 and the 'animal skin courier' was Paul Hawkins, an extremely colourful character, who had some racing experience in Africa, and subsequently in Europe, including the 1967 Le Mans. He will be encountered again in even more bizarre circumstances a few pages later!

It is possible that the ERA and the Lotus passed each other somewhere on the high seas; David suggests in fact it was on the Suez Canal, and if so, not quite the high seas! R12B Hanuman II arrived at Tilbury docks in November 1962; it was collected by David and taken to a lock-up garage in Wrottesley Road, Harlesden, North London. When David was contacted by the shipping agent he was told that there was a car *and* a chassis. David thought the latter was a mistake, but the documents showed that it was part of the shipment and R12C thus made its initial re-appearance. Although Gillespie had indicated there would be some spares accompanying the car, he had not provided any detail. It was a little while before the significance of the spare chassis dawned on Bill and David (its reconstruction is dealt with in Chapter 4).

Maintaining the car: workshop adventures

It was not possible to do any detailed work on the car in Wrottesley Road so a search was made for more suitable premises. A lock-up garage was found underneath a block of flats off the Chelsea Embankment, near to Battersea Bridge. Although it was a secure location it was not ideal. Quite apart from its size, the approach was awkward, as it was not wide enough to get a transporter down, so the car had to be towed out in order to load up. On one occasion, just prior to a meeting the car was brought out on to the embankment rather late at night and started up. This did not promote good relations with the local

R12B Hanuman II in Wrottesley Road, north London in the autumn of 1962. David Kergon collected the car from the docks when it arrived back in the UK from southern Africa. The car still has the numbers on its tail from its last meeting in Rhodesia.

One of the unsolved mysteries from Bill's files: this is one of several monthly receipts for rent, dated 1966, to David at his then address in Bishop's Bridge Road, for a garage in Queens Gate Mews North and not the one in Lancaster Gate Mews, which everyone remembers! Perhaps it was an arrangement to suit the Agent, or an unintentional error or some more dubious reason that has been lost in the mists of time? The heading in regard to the 1851 Exhibition however, is fascinating! Each invoice was paid on time and the rental ended in December 1966.

constabulary or with the neighbours. So another search was made and with the help of the advertisement columns of *The Times* (in those days still on its front page) another garage was found.

The new location was in Lancaster Mews and was very nearly ideal. It was a three-car unit and the surrounding garages were being used by well-known motor sport personalities such as Jock Finlayson, who had worked for Seaman and Ramponi and Billy Rockell, who had been associated with both Seaman and Whitney Straight; there were also more 'modern' racers such as John Sprinzel and Charles Lucas. As Bill put it "whenever we were making a noise there was always someone making a worse one".

The one possible snag about the garage was its expense but Bill and David succeeded in persuading Sandy Skinner to rent one third of the space. Sandy was building his Phoenix G.N. Special in the course of which Bill lent him a hammer and screwdriver – both of which he wrecked! Many years later Bill recalled the occasion when this formidable special was first fired up. He claimed that, together with Peter Royer-Collard, they pushed Sandy in the car down the Mews, the engine fired and the car sped off – only to go straight on at the first corner and through a yellow front door and halfway up the staircase inside. Sandy stoutly denies this account and thinks two or even three stories have been run together "The G.N. started like a dream under the eyes of a P.C… About a year later I put the wooden Austin fairly harmlessly into a Ruston Mews garage door through over-reliance on the handbrake when I couldn't find any brake-fluid for a test".

Even if Sandy didn't assault the yellow front door, another of the motoring brigade, Malcolm "Boysy" Clube certainly did. He was mounted on a grass track motor bike and seemed to be everywhere that Bill raced, usually on his MV Agusta bike, the fairing of which was distinctively decorated with cameos of scantily clad females! He customarily sported one green and one red sock to remind him of port and starboard. "Boysy" had made a dramatic initial impression on Bill and his friends as the doors of his garage flew open and he staggered out having nearly gassed himself starting up his autogyro!

"Boysy" by no means exhausted the colourful life of Lancaster Mews. One Christmas when they were working late getting the car ready for the Boxing Day Brands meeting, they were invited for a Christmas drink by the lady who lived over the garage. The flat was smart and in keeping with the Aston Martin DB4 she ran. Drinks dispensed, conversation ensued and Peter, being more forward than Bill asked her what she did. She explained that she was a prostitute – an expensive one – and that she intended working for another five years and would then retire. This took them both back a bit but she was very nice and very attractive, Bill says!

R12B Hanuman II on its ex-John Sprinzel Ford F100 transporter in the Shelsley paddock. The twin rear wheels on the car were not a success, as modern rubber provided sufficient traction on single wheels. The twins added extra weight and made the ERA a much wider car to negotiate the narrow gradient.

These varied delights of the Mews were 'enjoyed' until 1968 when Bill purchased a house in Leafield, a village near Witney in Oxfordshire. Both R12B Hanuman II and the chassis of R12C were then moved to Leafield together with all the spares and workshop equipment and this remained their base for all the rest of Bill's racing life. The move to Leafield was carried out using R12B Hanuman II's transporter, which was an ex-United States Air Force Ford F100 previously owned by John Sprinzel. The back had been cut off behind the cab and an additional six feet welded into the chassis. Two steel channels were fitted to carry the ERA with a mechanical winch to get the car on and off. It was greatly tested when used for carrying the lathe from London to Leafield. David recalls that "the weight gently bent the F100's chassis en route. Repairs were effected on the A40 roadside by a helpful lorry driver with a blow torch and blocks under the chassis rails!"

Maintaining the car: the first major rebuild

However interesting the locale of the workshop, its basic rationale was to provide somewhere to work on the car and it was quickly apparent to Bill and David that Hanuman II required a lot of attention. The car was both severely under-powered and not very reliable. On the first occasion it was raced, at a Boxing Day Brands Hatch meeting, it finished last and even allowing for driver inexperience, the main problem was its poor power output. Some work was undertaken on the top end of the engine and on the brakes in 1963-4, but at the end of 1964

Some mementos from Bill's first season with Hanuman II. They include his 1963 Medical Certificate and RAC Licence together with competitor badges from Snetterton meetings in May and August 1963.

it was decided that a comprehensive rebuild was what it really required.

The work was master-minded by Bill, but a great deal of time and effort was put in by various friends and associates, many of whom were drawn from Bill and David's fellow apprentices at Smiths Industries. Those who came along to work on the car were doing so very much for the love of it: at the end of an evening they might get a pie and chips and a pint, otherwise their reward lay in restoring a fine piece of engineering. Peter Royer-Collard (already met with) and Peter Rush were two such friends who laboured long and hard on this important rebuild, which was probably the first time R12B Hanuman II had been completely stripped down since it was recreated by Stan Holgate and the White Mouse Garage. When Brian Jordan from the magazine *Sporting Motorist* visited Lancaster Mews he noted that the rebuild had already been in progress for more than a year. Jordan reported that on average two people had been working on the car for three evenings a week and one whole day at the weekend, all of which added up to a very large number of man hours by the time the rebuild was finished.

One of the important changes made during the rebuild was to fit a B type inlet-manifold in place of the C type. As we noted in Chapter One, during the Hampshire/Murray ownership the Zoller blower was discarded and a Jamieson substituted. But the C type manifold was left in place and it did not make a very happy match with the new supercharger. It led to fuel starvation, particularly on No. 2 cylinder resulting in a large number of burnt pistons. The B type manifold produced some important improvements: the engine ran evenly, the mixture was correct and fuel consumption moderated.

During the time that Hanuman II was at Lancaster Mews, David and Bill were approached by Autokits, who wanted to use the car as a basis for a model kit. Accordingly, Hanuman II was measured up and the resultant kit was marketed from 1965. It was made of white metal to a scale of 1:24 and included rubber simulated tyres. It had to be glued together and could be painted in whatever colour suited. It is widely acknowledged as one of the most successful attempts to model an ERA, largely because it succeeds in capturing the basic shape and proportions of the car in a way that has defeated others. It isn't perfect: there are some curious omissions such as the rear view mirrors, and by modern standards some things, like the wheels, look a trifle crude (and show three rather than two-eared hub caps). But these are minor flaws in an overall design that is very good.

The Autokits ERA model which was based on R12B. Subsequently supplied by Wills Finecast it remained in production for many years. This particular example is Bill's own.

R12B Hanuman II's racing activity in the 1960s

At the time when Bill and David began to race the car in 1963, and even more so by 1966, when the major rebuild had been completed, ERAs were firmly established as a leading element in historic racing. The Vintage Sports Car Club (VSCC) was the major British club providing events for cars like the ERA. Its pattern of meetings, which took shape in the 1950s, consisted of three circuit meetings – two at Silverstone and one at Oulton Park – together with the annual hill climb at Prescott. Other venues with which the Club is now associated such as Donington, Cadwell and Shelsley Walsh were added to the list in the 1970s and 1980s. There were other clubs which provided some suitable events such as the Aston Martin Owner's Club and occasionally continental circuits also featured races for historic cars.

One of the VSCC's most important races was for the Richard Seaman trophies – one of which was for historic cars, one for vintage. When these trophies were first competed for in 1950, an ERA won the historic trophy but for the first few years the Bourne cars were fairly thin on the ground. From 1956 onwards more ERAs were entered and by the 1960s there were usually seven or eight competing, three of which invariably filled the leading places.

Many of Bill and David's racing contemporaries acquired their ERAs in the late 1950s and early 1960s: they included people such as Donald Day, Sid Day, Peter Waller, Patrick Lindsay, Sandy Murray, Dudley

Originally the ERA Club had been founded by Rivers Fletcher in 1936, and was revived in 1964. The ticket and menu for the 1965 Annual Dinner can be seen, the latter attended by leading ERA figures from the pre- and post-war period; David Kergon was secretary of the revived club for some years.

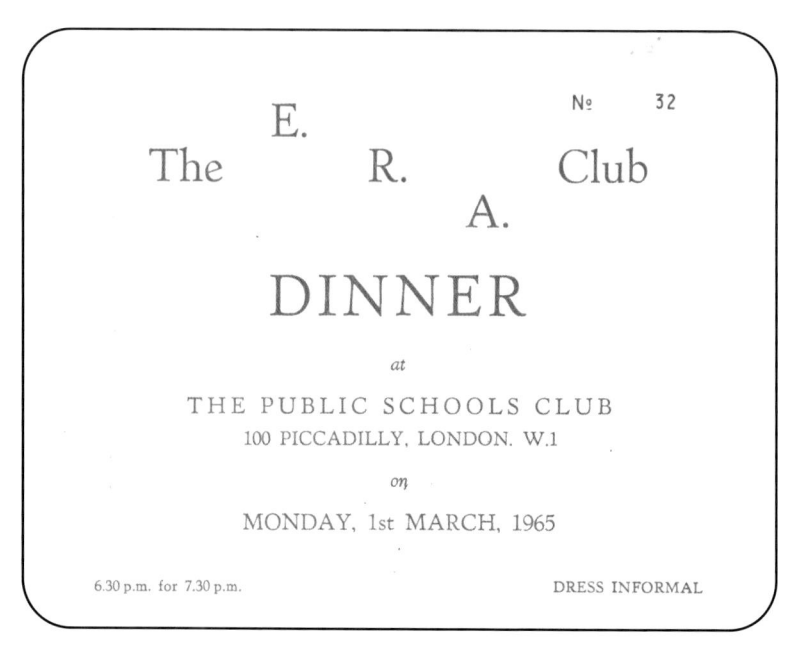

The E. R. A. Club

№ 32

DINNER

at

THE PUBLIC SCHOOLS CLUB
100 PICCADILLY, LONDON. W.1

on

MONDAY, 1st MARCH, 1965

6.30 p.m. for 7.30 p.m.   DRESS INFORMAL

Gahagan, Martin Morris and Patrick Marsh. Nearly all were, like Bill and David, owners, drivers and mechanics. Patrick Lindsay was an exception as he did employ someone else to look after his car but as this was Douglas Hull, who had been a prominent ERA owner and driver himself, his expertise was available to the new generation of ERA owners.

Both Bill and David stress the importance of the help and assistance they received from many of those mentioned above. It is clear that a key feature in the vitality of ERAs over the years has been the existence of a shared 'culture', a body of knowledge and experience about every aspect of the cars' design and performance. The opportunity to discuss common problems and swap experiences has been a big factor in encouraging people to keep the cars active and competitive. Another advantage of a group sharing an interest in a particular marque is the opportunity to spread the cost of specially manufactured parts. The price of a new cylinder block is likely to be lower if it has come from a small batch rather than cast as a one-off.

Bill and David's partnership was based on the principle of sharing all aspects of the car – ownership, costs, preparation and driving. In practice this had to be adapted to changing circumstances. After David had finished his training he went to work for Smiths Industries in Germany which meant he could not take an equal part in preparation. Bill and David also developed different preferences for competition work. David felt happier with hill climbs whereas Bill always preferred

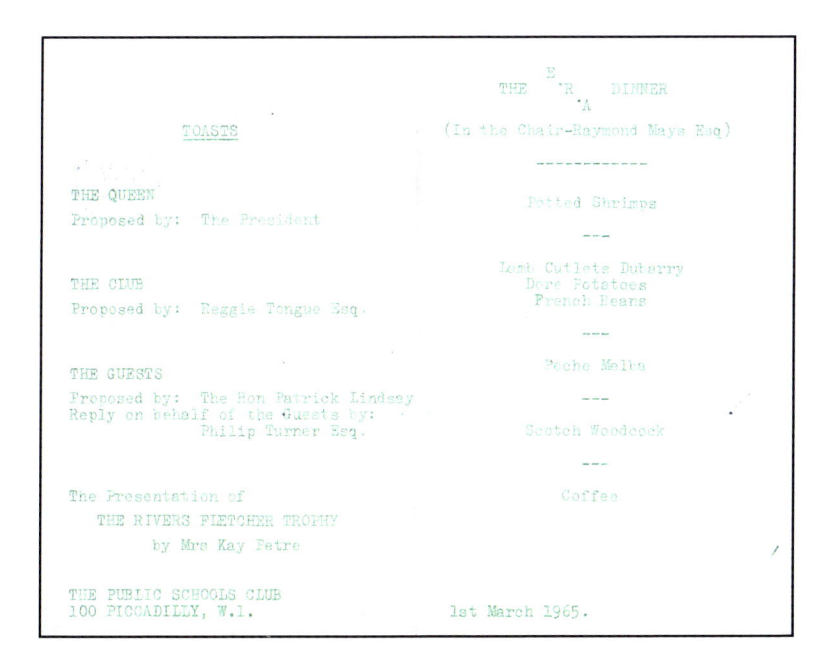

```
                              THE  E R A  DINNER

            TOASTS              (In the Chair-Raymond Mays Esq)
                                ---------------

THE QUEEN
Proposed by:  The President         Potted Shrimps
                                      ---

                                    Lamb Cutlets Dubarry
THE CLUB                            Dore Potatoes
Proposed by:  Reggie Tongue Esq.    French Beans
                                      ---

                                    Peche Melba
THE GUESTS
Proposed by:  The Hon Patrick Lindsey  ---
Reply on behalf of the Guests by:
              Philip Turner Esq.    Scotch Woodcock
                                      ---

The Presentation of                 Coffee
   THE RIVERS FLETCHER TROPHY
        by Mrs Kay Petre

THE PUBLIC SCHOOLS CLUB
100 PICCADILLY, W.1.              1st March 1965.
```

R12B at British Week, Düsseldorf, West Germany. Hanuman II had an interesting 'extramural' experience when it formed part of a group of British cars in an exhibition of UK technology. The car was flown back from Düsseldorf and briefly fired-up to run along the airport apron – possibly the first time an ERA had been heard in Germany since pre-War days?

circuit events. David's preferences for the hills reflected what many others have felt about their virtues: "Hill climbs were you versus the clock: no one to bump into or keep out of the way of". On the circuits he always felt slightly apprehensive: "Early on you learn your limitations by being passed at Woodcote by Patrick Lindsay in *Remus* when you were sliding around and really trying!" Bill had reservations about the hills: the racing experience is very brief and is a big strain on an ERA gearbox.

Obviously moving from a Brooklands Riley to an ERA was quite a big step: on the back of a photo of Bill at his first outing with the car he wrote "scared the trousers off myself". No doubt, but the fact that Hanuman II was considerably under-powered eased the transition. ERAs, when they

Bill's first race in R12B, AMOC's Martini Trophy meeting at Silverstone, July 1963. Bill wrote on the back of the photo: "Scared the trousers off myself!" He is wearing a duffle coat to keep warm and is talking to Martin Morris. The car is little changed from the Wrottesley Road photo save for some unorthodox three-eared hub caps. Freeman's well-known ex-Horsfall Aston Martin is in the background.

Early days at Brands Hatch (note the lion in situ still), Bill is being pushed to the marshalling area by David and a fellow Smiths' apprentice, Bob Walters. The fashionable matching headgear perhaps inspired by Mike Hawthorn?

are working properly, are quite powerful racing cars but they are not intrinsically difficult to drive. David was struck by its "rock hard suspension and lightning response to the throttle and the positive, direct but light steering". You certainly needed one hundred per cent concentration and David never understood how pre-war drivers like Bira were able to cope with races lasting two or three hours, over roads that were in a considerably worse condition than the current, smooth tarmac of British circuits.

By the time the car had been rebuilt for the start of the 1966 season, Bill had acquired a great deal of knowledge about the ins and outs of an ERA. After that initial rebuild he had more than thirty years further

Bill at Crystal Palace in September 1963. This was Bill's first drive at the south London circuit and he looks suitably determined. Hanuman II raced again on a number of occasions at Crystal Palace.

These two photographs form an interesting contrast in the story of R12B Hanuman II: The first is similar to the other early ones showing the ERA as it returned from South Africa. The second depicts the car following its major re-build in 1965/6. In the first photo, taken at Snetterton in 1963, the lion is rampant on the scuttle and the very large lever-arm hydraulic shock absorbers with the connecting bar and steel plates are still in place.

In the second photo, taken at the 1966 Daily Express Trophy meeting at Silverstone, the lion has disappeared in the repaint and has been replaced by a much more discreet Thai flag. The ironmongery surrounding the shock absorbers has also gone. There are some changes to the driver as well: a more modern crash helmet and a set of racing overalls have replaced the older helmet, shirt and pullover.

Concours era: Bill and David regularly entered Hanuman II for the concours competition at VSCC Oulton Park in the late 1960s and early 1970s. Bill is doing his concours parade lap in 1966 with an immaculate-looking R12B. The bridge spanning the starting grid at Oulton was dismantled some years ago. Later in the day Bill was runner-up in the Seaman Historic Trophy Race.

Geoffrey Kergon also entered his Rolls 20/25 in this event and so the challenge in the one lap parade was for Bill to do two laps of the circuit to Geoffrey's one... "the racer won't go that slow, mister!". On another occasion it was reported ... "For the concours parade, I joined the other nine people in Geoff Kergon's Rolls 20 limousine which put in a particularly gripping standing start lap of the circuit in 8 mins 33.5 secs. Our couriers on this tour were Messrs. Morris and Kergon D., who pointed out the various spots where they had suffered moments of drama in Hanuman over the years."

fettling, not only of his own cars, but of a number of other ERAs as well. His considered view is that the basic design is very sound and provided ERAs are carefully maintained they present few serious problems. If there is a weak link it's the gearbox and that means it is advisable to have a spare on hand as you can never be sure when it will let you down. Brakes on the A and B type cars also need careful adjustment and there used to be a danger of bending the rear axle under violent acceleration with resultant damage to the crown wheels and pinions. In recent years appropriate tolerances have been machined and this is no longer a problem.

After the 1965/6 rebuild, Hanuman II was a much improved car in every respect. Its appearance was praised – "it comes to our meetings in truly concours condition" (*VSCC Bulletin*, Summer 1966). Bill and David did in fact enter it for a number of the concours at Oulton Park which were run as part of the Seaman meeting and in 1967 it was awarded the second prize in the Concours d'Etat. Looking the part is fine but of course the key test for a racing car is its performance on the

David Kergon's '15 minutes of fame'! He has just won the 1968 Seaman Historic Trophy Race. David claimed that he won the race, not by his skill but by the fact that the float chamber came loose on R1A so that Tony Merrick couldn't accelerate out of right hand corners!

Silverstone in 1967; David is in the driver's seat with Bill, Gordon Allan and Peter 'Lofty' Royer-Collard providing the horse power. David still owns the Les Leston crash helmet!

track. Good results began to accumulate here as well: Bill finished second in the 1966 Seaman Historic Trophy and David won the race in 1968. David describes his victory as his '15 minutes of fame' and, as is sometimes the way, few photographs appear to have survived to commemorate this very satisfying win. There *is* one rather blurred shot of David returning to the paddock with Bill riding on the tail wearing a trilby hat and holding the laurel wreath in his hand! Subsequently the well-known artist Roy Nockolds completed a painting of David coming up Deer's Leap with Lodge corner in the background, which is a much-valued souvenir of that occasion.

Prior to David's Seaman win Bill had collected a couple of 'firsts' himself, though as these were in races open to post-war cars as well, they weren't outright victories but first among the pre-war cars. Bill's first overall win came in July 1969 with victory in the Pre-War Allcomers' Scratch Race, Hanuman II sounding "magnificent" according to Sandy Skinner who was the *VSCC Bulletin*'s scribe for the day. In the same year Bill drove at Prescott for the first time in the VSCC's annual hill climb. Reflecting the preferences already noted it had been David who had piloted Hanuman II to the top in previous years. Bill's best run on this first foray was 48.92, good enough for a class second but over the next twenty years he speeded up considerably with some outstanding times, as we shall see in the following chapter.

Naturally, things didn't always go right; there were occasions when mechanical maladies or the odd 'excursion' led to non-starts, retirements

One does not need too much muscle power to drive an ERA, but this picture might give a different impression. It shows a very young Bill with a wide grin on his face, obviously enjoying the day and the results of his labours!

or a finish way down the field. In the early part of 1967 Hanuman II's crankshaft failed at Silverstone and following its replacement, Bill then broke a half-shaft during practice for the Seaman race in June. He was able to borrow a replacement from Douglas Hull and fit it in what was described as an "astonishingly short space of time". In the race itself, having stalled on the start-line, he made good progress through the field until he was baulked by a back marker at Island Bend: "He was forced to brake violently and spun up the road towards Esso at about 100 mph, fortunately without collecting anything on the way. He described it afterwards in similar words to those used on another occasion by Harry Rose, who remarked that only God and his laundryman knew how frightened he was" (*VSCC Bulletin*, Autumn 1967)

Foreign parts with Hanuman II

Although the great majority of Hanuman II's competition work in the 1960s was in the U.K. it did include an occasional overseas outing. In fact in 1966 there were two meetings only a month or so apart – firstly at Rouen in north-west France and secondly at Karlskoga in Sweden. By contrast with the familiarity of Silverstone or Oulton these foreign circuits were more or less unknown and they involved far more travel than U.K. events. Perhaps not surprisingly they are well-remembered though more for off-course activity than the actual racing!

The Rouen race took place at the Les Essarts circuit, a most attractive and challenging venue. Much enjoyed by Hanuman II and his crew was the French attitude to motor sport described by Denis Jenkinson of *Motor Sport*: "There is no problem in France if you want to try out your

David in the paddock at Rouen in 1966.

racing car, you put a number on the back and belt off up the road. Saturday was a riotous day with ERAs, Bugattis, Delage and M. Pichon's Le Mans Delahaye dicing up and down the road to Rouen".

After the race in which Bill finished second he was persuaded by John Bolster, who had been commentating, to venture forth to Paris to sample the night life along with Bolster and Paul Hawkins ('the animal skin courier'). The evening's events, more or less in order were a good meal, a strip joint, Paul Hawkins ending up on the stage in a stripping routine and finally Paul and the stripper leaving the club, both stark naked, in his Ferrari! Bill completes the tale: "I saw Paul about a month later and he just said he had had a very nice few days in the south of France. When I remonstrated that he had left John and me to pick up the tab *and* find our way back to England without a car, he simply gave me an impish smile and walked away!" Fortunately, prior to Bill's departure for Paris, Hanuman II's safe return to the U.K. had been entrusted to David Kergon's brother, Geoffrey, who had the ERA in tow behind his Rolls 20/25.

So far as the trip to Sweden was concerned it's again the events surrounding the meeting that seem to have lodged in the memory. During the ferry crossing from Hull to Gothenburg Patrick Lindsay and Hamish Moffatt entertained their fellow drivers – and quite a number of the other passengers – with a vivid account of the Sydney Marathon when Patrick's eight-litre Bentley had overturned in the mountains of Afghanistan. By chance, some tribesmen on horseback appeared, armed to the teeth. They were able to right the car and release Patrick. It was then discovered the leader of the horsemen had been at Eton with Patrick so they were able to summon further help and return him to hospital in London. Literally an example of the old boy network to the rescue!

Rouen 1966, just after the flag has fallen: George Burton is first off in the Sunbeam 'Tiger', followed by Bill Summers in his P3 Alfa Romeo, then Peter Waller and Bill in R9B and R12B Hanuman II respectively. Waller ran out the winner with Bill coming second and Patrick Lindsay in R5B Remus third.

> Map.
> Carnet / ERA.
> Green Card / Lorry.
> Helmet.
> Goggles.

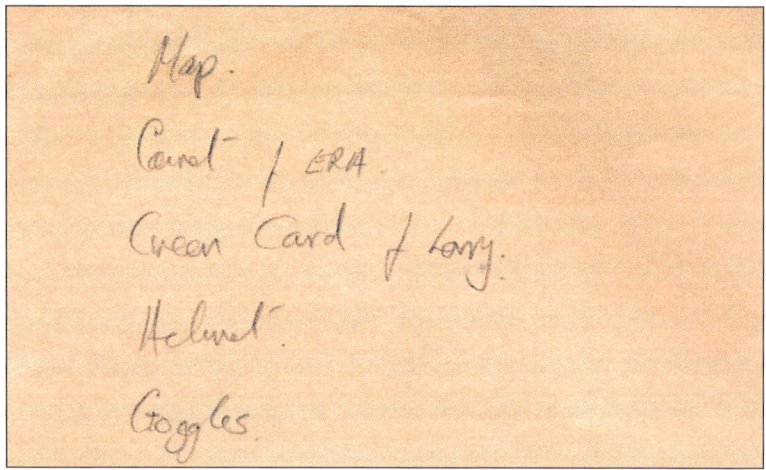

This is David's 'must take' list for the Swedish trip to Karslkoga. Note that no mention is made of personal necessities or any other items. This list makes an interesting comparison to the current baggage – equipment personnel and transportation of the current F1 era.

The Douglas Hull XK140 with Remus on its trailer follows R12B on the F100, with Hamish Moffat's Type 35 on its trailer awaiting documentation to be stamped and thence embarkation for Gothenburg at Hull. A green carnet was required on these trips abroad and there was considerable trouble with Customs later in the UK as by mistake they did not get the document stamped on departure from Sweden and the officials in the UK took some convincing that they had in fact not sold Hanuman in Europe.

Once they had landed in Gothenburg, David recalls following Douglas Hull, who was towing *Remus* (for Patrick Lindsay), at very high speed. Douglas was using a modified XK140 as a towing vehicle and David was driving the F100 ex-Sprinzel truck; complete with British Rail air horns these two ensembles must have made a fine – and unfamiliar – spectacle for any Swedes by the roadside! It only remains to add that Bill finished 6th in the race, but more than that has not survived!

End of the beginning?

Although dividing history up into decades is often a highly artificial business there were some significant changes for Bill, David and Hanuman II during the 1970s, so we take up the story in a new chapter. There wouldn't have been a continuing story if the option to sell Hanuman had been chosen. In the late 1960s Neil Corner sounded out Bill and David about a possible part-exchange deal with his P3 Alfa, number 5006, which was one of the 1932 ex-works cars. Although the deal had some attractions, they decided, in David's words, "to stay with

Two photographs taken at the Bugatti Owners' Club meeting at Prescott in 1968. Bill is talking to Rivers Fletcher in front of R12B Hanuman II.

Rivers is in the driving seat with Peter Rush (in cap) and Peter Royer-Collard, two fellow apprentices at Smiths who had both made major contributions to R12B's rebuild in 1965/6.

In late June 1971 Bill and David took Hanuman II to Cornwall to demonstrate it to Princess Chula. It was in part a thank offering for various parts she had made available for the reconstruction of R12C. Her letter to David is reproduced and it is interesting to see her reference to 're-organising Romulus' – a theme taken up in Chapter Five. The picture shows Hanuman II on the warming-up jack with David in the driving seat and Bill alongside. No racing numbers, of course, this was strictly a demonstration!

TREDETHY
BODMIN
CORNWALL
TELEPHONE ST MABYN 232

4.7.71.

Dear Mr Keigen —

I must thank you and Mr Morris very much for the enormous pleasure you gave to me in bringing Hanuman down, and displaying him so expertly, last Sunday. I never dreamed you would have been able to restore the car with such perfection. You have both given an enormous amount of enthusiasm and devotion to this special cult, and I am delighted the results have been so gratifying.

everyone else enjoyed the display enormously, and regarded themselves as highly privileged to see hear and smell such a sight.

I hope you had a good run back, and I shall look forward to arranging all the details of Voisin and re-organising Romulus. Thank you both so much.

Yours sincerely

Elisabeth Chakrabongse

Bill's armband was for September 1963 when the meeting was organised by the British Racing and Sports Car Club.

what we knew and had learnt about". Neil subsequently bought ERA R4D from Peter Brewer, and the Alfa went to a Japanese enthusiast.

As David's comment indicates, by the end of the 1960s he and Bill had learnt much about ERAs in general and Hanuman II in particular. When they bought the car in 1962 they knew little about ERAs and their individual histories but by the late 1960s they had become thoroughly familiar with them. Obviously the complete strip-down in 1965-6 had been a key stage in learning about the car and the rebuild incorporated important modifications, such as the B type manifold, which cured many of the weaknesses that had shown up in the first year or two of racing. Both had learnt to drive the car during the course of which they had developed different preferences – Bill's for circuit events, David for the hills – and both had secured some good results. How did things change in the decades that followed?

Judging by Bill's headwear this rather enigmatic photo is from the late 1960s. It shows R12B's hydraulic brakes and the small silver Hanuman motif attached to the top left corner of the radiator grille.

The programme is for 1971, the penultimate year of circuit racing at Crystal Palace, when Bill competed in the Seven Seas Fellowship Challenge Trophy.

Chapter Three

Bill and Hanuman II – from the 1970s to the 1990s

The changing context of historic racing

The previous chapter dealt with the first eight years of Bill and David's racing activity, whereas this chapter covers a period nearly four times as long. The first few years with a racing car have a particular significance because of the importance of initial impressions and experience. Unless something fairly fundamental occurs, succeeding decades tend to have similar characteristics to those of the initial period. In part, but only in part, that describes the situation for Bill and David; the other part of the story is that there were some important changes during these three decades both in their racing partnership and in the world of historic racing.

One element of continuity was that most of Hanuman II's racing took place in events organized by the VSCC. But that calendar did not remain set in stone – additional circuit events were promoted at Donington, Cadwell and Mallory; and on the hills Shelsley, Wiscombe and Loton were added to the Club's fixtures. There were also significant new organising bodies offering additional opportunities for historic cars such as the JCB Championship, subsequently the Lloyds and Scottish, and these also involved commercial or sponsorship finance. Such funding was also a feature of a large-scale meeting at Silverstone devoted to historic racing where first Coys, and then Chrysler, acted as the major sponsor. Finally there was Goodwood – firstly the Festival of Speed from 1993 and then the re-opening of the old circuit with the Revival meetings which started in 1998.

There was a stepping-up of European events too – with meetings at Zandvoort and Nurburgring becoming annual events in the 1980s. The Historic Grand Prix Cars Association (HGPCA) was founded in 1979 and it has had an important role in organising some of the European events as well as putting on races in the U.K.

Sponsorship money, more events and the general rise in asset values (the latter especially marked during the 1980s) contributed to raise the profile of two issues, 'authenticity' and 'eligibility'. The first revolves around whether certain cars are what they purport to be; often whether certain 'genuine', 'real' or 'authentic' elements can be combined together and assume a certain identity. 'Eligibility' wrestles with what kinds of modern materials should be allowed and in what quantities in vital components such as engine, tyres and bodywork. Neither of these issues was absolutely new, indeed they are surely intrinsic to any competition activity involving 'historic' cars but they do seem to have become more troublesome in recent decades. Clubs such as the VSCC have devoted a considerable amount of time to defining what is acceptable.

A further indication of change in the post-1960s has been a whole cluster of safety concerns. These were originally brought to the fore in Formula One but once accepted as legitimate at that level, such issues resonated throughout the whole of motor sport. There have been changes in circuit design and 'architecture' with grassed areas, gravel traps, Armco and increased chicanes as well as tougher regulations about car design, what drivers must wear and the ground rules for running meetings.

Bill Morris and the changing context of racing

Before we look at the impact of some of the changes just outlined, an important 'domestic' change must be noted. David and Bill's racing partnership continued for the first half of the 1970s but was dissolved at the end of 1974. From 1975 onwards Bill assumed sole ownership of both Hanuman II and the part-rebuilt R12C. David's work commitments and a domestic move to Suffolk made his continuing involvement impracticable. When they bought R12B their partnership had been formally registered by a solicitor and while this was probably unusual it turned out to be prudent, especially as it spelt out how the partnership should be dissolved. It meant a full and agreed settlement was made at the point of dissolution, thus avoiding the kind of disputes that have arisen in other cases of shared ownership.

The impact of the various changes sketched out above was mainly felt by Bill, as they chiefly took shape in the latter 1970s and especially during the 1980s. Bill didn't find all of them welcome, indeed some were certainly a 'pain', though he recognised that if you wanted to continue racing they had to be accommodated. When he judged that it was worth 'fighting the good fight', he entered the public lists to do so. One example was the introduction of roll-over hoops for historic cars which the RAC MSA was rumoured to be considering in the mid-1980s. Bill was against the idea and he wrote to *Motor Sport* arguing that it would make cars like ERAs *more* rather than *less* dangerous. There was other opposition too, and the idea was dropped.

Two shots of Bill at Prescott in R12B. The second one is taken at the start of his 1988 record breaking run. Note the early electrical technology for the timing equipment both with the hockey stick and Dexion pylon to the rear.

On the positive side, Bill welcomed the expansion of the VSCC programme, especially when it embraced new circuits such as Cadwell which he particularly enjoyed. The VSCC first used Cadwell in 1976 and as Chapter 5 relates Bill was mainly at the wheel of Romulus that year but he drove Hanuman II there on many other occasions. In 1979 Donington came onto the calendar and Bill won the Nuffield Trophy race in that opening year and again in 1986 and 1988. In the 1930s all the Nuffield races had been held at Donington and the trophy awarded to Bira for his victory in 1938 was subsequently presented to the VSCC by Narisa Chakrabongse. So Bill and Hanuman II were a singularly appropriate combination as the first names on the cup.

Bill didn't take advantage of the new hills in the VSCC's programme such as Shelsley and Wiscombe because as we have said in Chapter 2 in general he didn't find the hills very attractive. Prescott was an exception, in large part because it was very close to Leafield. Even so he wasn't brimming over with enthusiasm saying in 1972 "It's like driving up a drain" (!). After his fairly modest beginning there in 1969, Bill did not return until 1976 by which time he was more than four seconds quicker with a class-winning time of 44.76. Five years later he was recording 43.32 which brought him FTD and a new hill record for Pre-War cars and in 1988 there was a further significant improvement with his best-ever time of 42.39 which was another class record (in the twenty years since then only Duncan Ricketts has done a faster climb in a 1500cc ERA). It should also be recorded that Prescott turned out to be an extremely important place in his personal life as it was where he first met Victoria Read with whom he established a happy and mutually supportive companionship which led to marriage some years later.

So far as the vexed issues of 'authenticity' and 'eligibility' were concerned, Bill's aim with Hanuman II was to keep faith with the car's original specification. Such an aim allowed for a number of developments, three of which are worth noting. The first was the fitting of a limited slip differential, which various other ERAs had adopted, in some cases before the Second World War. It certainly altered the car's handling, especially in wet weather and therefore a period of 'driver retraining' was required. Martin Morris in reporting on the Paul Ricard meeting in 1980 commented that "Bill Morris would have finished much higher up than 12th if he'd not become giddy from so many spins, for which his excuse was that he was still learning how to drive with a ZF". Once mastered, it did have the requisite effect of improving starts and cornering.

The second development was to lighten the car. Bill carried this out during 1985/6, and the beneficial result was described in a report on the opening Silverstone meeting of 1986: "In fifth place was Bill Morris reaping the benefit of an eighteen month rebuild of R12B Hanuman II aimed at losing weight and resulting in a loss of two cwt. (100 kg) from the car, 19 pounds from the driver and two seconds from his own best lap time". This considerable slimming down was achieved in various ways. One example concerned the shock absorbers. When the car came back from Africa it had a pair of De Rams together with original Hartfords at the rear and lever hydraulic Armstrong dampers at the front. Bill subsequently acquired some aluminium bodied De Rams which he put on the front to replace the hydraulics. However these six dampers totted up to 69 lbs. As part of the lightening exercise the De Rams were abandoned and replicas of proper ERA Hartfords were substituted; the four

Hanuman II in Bill's workshop at Leafield during its major rebuild in 1985/6. The Hartford shock absorbers which replaced the De Rams can be seen with the back axle detached from the chassis.

R12B Hanuman II's first appearance (below) following its 1985/6 rebuild. Bill is duelling with Neil Corner in the ERA-Delage: they finished sixth and seventh in the first Patrick Lindsay Trophy Race (1986).

Hartfords weighed just under 20 pounds – a saving of nearly fifty pounds on the previous arrangement. Other aspects that received the weight – loss treatment were the radiator, the fuel tank and the wheels.

The third development involved adapting the Armstrong-Siddeley gearbox to give five forward speeds. The idea was to provide a lower first gear which would be especially helpful on take-off both on the circuits and at hill climbs. Bill had become very knowledgeable about ERA gearboxes and took over the business of Cyril Turnell in the mid-1980s (see Chapter 7). Turnell, who operated in very basic premises in Nuneaton – "out of his garden shed" was Bill's description – played a vital part for many years in keeping ERAs active. Martin Morris, writing in 1984 commented on how "we have all relied far too long on our marvellous friend Cyril Turnell to sort out our gearboxes when they go wrong" and he recalled an occasion when Peter Waller had stripped a gearbox and everything fell out, "gear teeth, needle rollers, brass filings, the lot all came tumbling out and Peter said I'm sorry Martin this is a job for Cyril!".

Bill was influenced in his gearbox modification by a climate of what he called 'ultra-competitiveness' which prevailed in the late 1980s and early 1990s and resulted in what he described as "people getting up to all sorts of mischief" with their cars. This was one of the points at which the VSCC, in response to the 'mischief', decided to tighten the eligibility rules and that meant the end of the five-speed gearbox.

The 1970s and the 1980s: Hanuman II's racing activity

From 1970-1973 the car was still shared between David and Bill and Hanuman II remained active with the balance of the driving varying over the four seasons. For example in 1971 Bill had seven races and David four, whereas the following year David competed in nine races and Bill only in one, but the following year the advantage swung back in Bill's favour. In 1975, Bill's first year as sole owner, he took part in six races. An important change occurred in 1976 when Bill became responsible for the maintenance and the driving of ERA R2B, Narisa Chakrabongse's Romulus. This very interesting episode is dealt with in Chapter 5 and although Bill continued to drive Hanuman II, it had a lower profile in his hands over the next couple of years. Its semi-vacant driving seat was filled by Bill's brother Ben Morris and the spectacle of the brothers racing alongside each other, both in former Bira cars, made quite an impression on fellow drivers, Martin Morris declaring at the 1976 Oulton Park "Bloody white mice everywhere!"

In 1978 Bill took Hanuman II to Australia and this initial experience of racing on the other side of the world led to a number of subsequent

VSCC Silverstone: David Kergon found time to stick out his tongue at freelance photographer Michael Ware at Copse. He later said that it was quicker to do that than to wave at him!

similar expeditions – in 1983/4, 1988, 1993/4 and 2003 (in this last case it was with R12C). When Bill returned from his first Australian visit he had a very active season in 1979 to bring the 1970s to a close but began the new decade with a quiet year in 1980. For the remainder of the 1980s he averaged half a dozen meetings with the important exception of the mid-1980s when the car was withdrawn for the major rebuild referred to above. 1988 was also unusual with the car in Thailand at the beginning of the year and Australia at the end and with a more than usually busy U.K. season in between.

The period from 1970 to 1988 (the last U.K. competition season for Bill in Hanuman II) involves nearly twenty years of historic racing and obviously there were certain similarities from one season to another. Equally, as we have already outlined, the context of racing was changing with new or modified tracks, changes in the regulations, new organisers and promoters of historic racing and fresh challenges to the leading ERAs and their drivers. It's worth highlighting some of the distinctive features of Bill's experience during the 1970s and 1980s by looking at various aspects of his competition activity – in Britain, Australia and Thailand – and then at various important decisions he made – particularly about rebuilding the car, who else might drive it and finally whether it should be sold.

Racing experiences 1: British historic racing

Until the development of major historic meetings at Silverstone and Goodwood the VSCC was the pre-eminent organiser of historic racing in Britain. Much energy was expended by owners and drivers of vintage

Silverstone 1988: Bill in very close company with Ludovic Lindsay in R5B Remus and John Venables-Llewelyn in R4A. They battled away for second, third and fourth throughout the Patrick Lindsay Race. The VSCC Bulletin *commented: "The fight for second place reached a crescendo at the end of lap five when the trio appeared round Woodcote in line abreast, an exercise of which Patrick Lindsay would have heartily approved!" They finished as they are pictured… with Remus and R4A so close that the timekeepers could not separate them!*

and historic cars in trying to win its major awards, among the most important of which were the Richard Seaman trophies. David and Bill's first Seaman, in 1964, saw David bring R12B home in fourth place. Bill's first Seaman drive was in 1966 with Hanuman II fresh from its major rebuild and Bill finished a very satisfied runner-up to Peter Waller.

As described in the previous chapter David won the race in 1968 and rather surprisingly this is the only occasion (so far) that Hanuman II has carried off the Historic Trophy. In fact whether there was something in the north-west water that didn't suit the car, we can't tell, but it did seem somewhat more prone to problems at Oulton than on other circuits. In 1970 Bill had all the bearings go, for the second time in a month and the VSCC scribe confirmed that it was not Bill's day when he reported the post-meeting drink at Little Budworth: "… a large flock of starlings flew overhead. Instinctively all present put their hands over their beer mugs. All, that is, except for Bill Morris, who got his priorities wrong and put his hand on his head. As it says in the Bible, the lot fell on Morris…"

Even if the number of Seaman non-starts and retirements was greater than Bill would have liked, when all went well there were some good results. He was runner-up in 1986 and third in 1976 (with R2B),

Bill out-accelerates Anthony Mayman (No. 5; R4D) and Ludovic Lindsay (nearest camera in R5B Remus) at Donington in September 1988. Bill was second overall and winner of the Nuffield Trophy in the Shuttleworth and Nuffield Trophies Race. In the All-comers Race, later in the programme, he finished third.

1979 and 1982 and fourth in 1983. His races in 1982 and 1986 involved close tussles with Brian Classic, driving R2A; their battle for third place in 1982 lasted the whole race with only a few yards separating the two cars at the flag.

One memorable meeting which was outside the British mainland but only modestly so compared to the expeditions to Australasia and Thailand discussed below was a 1975 visit to the Republic of Ireland to race at Phoenix Park. In September 1975 an historic race – The Gold Leaf Trophy – was mounted for the first time. One report in the Irish press declared this event "was the most interesting of all the weekend's racing". One of its principal features was a race-long duel for third and fourth spots between Bill in Hanuman II and Patrick Lindsay in *Remus*. A commentator in *Autosport* thought "it was one of the finest spectacles I have yet witnessed. Historic cars do not look right on modern circuits. At Phoenix Park they were in their element and the sight of the two ERAs flashing between the trees with all the attendant sound effects, really demonstrated to me what motor racing should be all about" (*Autosport*, 23 October 1975).

From the vantage point of the twenty-first century it is clear that the 1980s were an intensely competitive period for racing cars of the 1930s. From the 1950s, when the VSCC first organised races for cars such as ERAs, there was a progressive build up in both quantative and qualitative terms which reached its peak in the mid and late 1980s. By then there was no problem in getting thirty cars on to the grid for the Pre-War All Comers races at Silverstone, which would typically include seven or eight ERAs, Monza and P3 Alfas, various Maseratis, T51 Bugattis, MGs and various interesting 'one-off' marques or specials. Fairly early in the 1990s these buoyant entries began to contract and only the Goodwood Revival and the biennial Monaco race now seem able to mobilise a comparable field.

So far as the ERA component was concerned, the trend in the 1970s and 1980s was for the 1500cc engined cars to upgrade their engines to two litres. Bill did not follow this route, resolutely sticking to Hanuman II's $1\frac{1}{2}$ litre unit. As such he was a front-runner among the 1500cc cars – whether ERA or any other marque – and he was able to mix it with the fastest two-litre ERAs. There was a vivid illustration of this in the 1988 Patrick Lindsay race when Bill was in very close competition with Ludovic Lindsay and John Venables-Llewelyn, both in two-litre ERAs: "The fight for second place reached a crescendo at the end of lap 5 when the trio appeared round Woodcote in line abreast, an exercise of which Patrick Lindsay would have heartily approved…"(*VSCC Bulletin*, Summer 1988) The mid-1980s was also the period in which there was a strong challenge to ERA dominance, whatever their engine size. The P3 Alfas of drivers like David Black and Rodney Felton were a major problem for the leading ERAs and there were some very rapid Maseratis as well driven by people such as Peter Hannen and Martin Stretton.

Racing experiences 2: competing on the other side of the world – the Australasian expeditions

Bill's Australian expeditions were started off by Jim McDonald, his first Australian friend who originally met up with Bill in 1973. A casual encounter at Silverstone, where he had gone to spectate, led to Jim having a few drinks with Bill followed by a meal and then a night at Bill's house in Leafield. Four and a half years later, in March 1978, Bill and Hanuman II were on the grid of the 50th anniversary Australian Grand Prix held at the Philip Island circuit. This was only the second time an ERA had appeared in Australia: Bill had been preceded by Peter

R12B is unloaded in Australia by Jim McDonald and friends.

There are no less than 45 entries for the 1978 Australian Jubilee Scratch Race (above); the great majority are cars of the 1920s and 1930s, though one 4CLT/48 Maserati represents cars from the early post-war years. The picture shows R12B on pole position, Joel Finn in R10B can be glimpsed on the right of the photo.

While waiting for the race to start and just as the one minute board was shown, Bill was startled to find a helmeted face peering into his – " Keep out of my way, boy!" boomed at him! This was his introduction to Lou Molina, who was right at the back of the grid in his little bright yellow Bugatti 'Buttercup'. Bill became a firm friend and admirer of the venerated local historic driver.

Vintage honors to Britain

By CHRIS de FRAGA

Briton Bill Morris, driving a 1937 English ERA imported for the race, won the Australian Grand Prix Jubilee Scratch Race at Phillip Island yesterday.

But Morris didn't have it all his own way.

Keven Shearer of South Australia, in a remarkable Model A Ford 1929 special, closed to within two seconds of the classic ERA in the 80 kilometre race.

But then the Ford, fitted with cross ply road tyres, spun in the wet and the ERA went on to an easy victory.

Stuart Saunders of Canberra, in a 1927 type 35C Bugatti, was third.

The race was one of the closest fought on the nine-event programme.

A second ERA, a 1936 model driven by Joel Finn, got water in its ignition and misfired throughout the race. Many of the vintage and veteran cars suffered water in their electrics.

The sights, smells and roars of the vintage racers drew a good crowd of more than 10,000 despite the rain.

Morris' win repeated the British victory in the first Australian Grand Prix in 1928 when Col. E. Waite won in an Austin 7.

John Virgo, in a 1951 Riley special, won the Historic Sports Car Scratch Race. David Lowe, driving his Nedloh, won the Historic Racing Cars Handicap and Bernard Bisseling, in a 100/4 Austin Healey from 1954, won the Historic Sports Car Handicap.

Noel Robson won the Historic Racing Cars Scratch Race in an MG TC.

Whitehead who had won the 1938 Australian Grand Prix with R10B.

A few days prior to the race the temperature was running at over 40 centigrade and Bill was worried about how the car would cope in such conditions. He had already made some changes to Hanuman II – effectively de-tuning it by reducing the compression ratio, fitting a lower blower drive and running it rich to avoid burning pistons. Fortunately on race day itself the temperature had receded and the race was actually run in the wet, as Jim McDonald said "Just the thing for a Pom and his car!"

There was a varied grid which included John Goddard and Stuart Saunders with Type 35C Bugattis, Rileys, Austin Sevens, MGs and Ford Specials. The race was run over fifty miles and Bill established a useful lead over his nearest rival Kevin Shearer, driving a Ford Special. Around half-distance Shearer began to close up, helped by his Pirelli radials which were giving him better grip in the rain than Bill's Dunlop Racing

Contemporary press report of Bill's Australian GP Scratch Race victory.

Two photos from the Australian GP of 1978. There was a great deal of water in the latter stages of the race and the Australian Prime Minister, Malcolm Fraser, is suitably weather-protected as he admires Hanuman's winning engine with Bill on his left. The PM then asked for a lap of the circuit in Stuart Saunders' Bugatti which had come third and hopped in for the ride!

variety. When Kevin was only two seconds behind Bill he had a spin which dropped him back and although Bill had a few lurid moments in the final laps he kept ahead of Shearer. By the time Bill took the chequered flag, he had lapped all but five of the other runners which, as Jim McDonald said, "was a great effort in the conditions and considering he had never driven on the track before the race".

One of Bill's fellow competitors had retired very early and parked his car at a convenient vantage point to watch the race. He subsequently reported: "When the race was over and I had been towed back to the pits I went over to congratulate Bill Morris. While I was there Kevin Shearer drove in the Model A Special and paused to offer his congratulations. "Oh," said Bill "I still had a bit in hand, you know!" And as Kevin got out of earshot, "Like hell, I did!" Clearly these events had an ethos all of their own, the aforesaid reporter noted that one driver in a desperate attempt to stop his car from chronic boiling "pulled off the track, pushed his car to the edge of the lake in the centre of the circuit, plunged waist deep into the water and replenished the radiator from his helmet!" (*VSCC Bulletin*, Summer 1978) What would the U.K. race stewards have made of that – perhaps given him a special award for enterprise or, more likely, suspended his licence?

Bill received his trophy from the Australian Prime Minister, Malcolm Fraser. Bill had a swig from the champagne-filled cup and Malcolm Fraser – at Bill's invitation – drank the rest! Bill's imbibing, moderate as it was, had an unfortunate effect as he wasn't allowed to run in a subsequent race.

Bill revisited Australia with Hanuman II in 1994/5. The car was despatched from England in September and Duncan Ricketts drove it in two events in November – some speed trials at Geelong where he made FTD for pre-war cars and at an historic race meeting at Wakefield Motorsport Park, where he finished first in all four races. The car remained in Australia until May 1995 when Bill himself drove it in three events at Winton in May 1995 picking up two firsts and a fourth. This was the last occasion on which Bill drove Hanuman II, some thirty-two years after his first race in it.

Bill made two further racing trips to Australia, in 1999/2000 and 2004 but on both these occasions it was with R12C. As the following chapter details, mechanical problems prevented participation in the first of these meetings but the second produced another crop of successful results with Duncan Ricketts at the wheel of R12C.

When Bill first went to Australia in 1978, he travelled on to visit New Zealand, but his first motor racing there didn't come until five years later, in 1983/4. Allan Bramwell was a key figure: in the 1970s he had formed the 'Country Gentleman Racing and Sports Car Club'. If this sounds a trifle refined, its terms of reference were very much down to earth. It sought to run races for 'proper' cars, defined at the committee's discretion and, as Bramwell emphasises, "no matter how good your car if you were considered a 'boring bastard' you weren't allowed to race". He adds that race meetings were invariably followed by a "serious piss-up, good food and a jazz band in a marquee. Bill thought those were perfect conditions". Bramwell who ran a successful scaffolding firm provided some sponsorship money for Bill which resulted in T shirts bearing the inscription 'Bramwell Scaffolding for Fast Erections'!

Bill and R12B went to New Zealand in November 1983 and remained there until March 1984, undertaking a number of competition events as well as sampling lots of slices of New Zealand life. A D-I-Y scaffolding twin-deck transporter with a Cooper twin on top and the ERA underneath was used to take the cars to Whenuapai.

Against a background of large aircraft Bill and Hanuman II are at the Whenuapai Wings and Wheels Classic Show held at the Auckland base of the Royal New Zealand Air Force in February 1984.

Dunedin or Russia? Bill is racing in 1984 on a circuit that used dockland roads. A large Russian ship is berthed in the background and crowd protection is no more than a single line of rope. Not surprisingly Bill found the experience "rather frightening". The grid was varied – a 4CLT Maserati, Cooper 1100s and 500s, a Cooper-Bristol, a replica Ferrari and various specials. Hanuman II was the oldest but was second quickest.

Bill off-duty in New Zealand and at a slightly slower pace than usual! He is driving a 1920 Case tractor and in the background is a 1908 traction engine.

Bill did a lot of racing during this first trip to New Zealand – which was, of course, the first time an ERA had ever been to the country. There was a meeting at Wigram just before Christmas, a street circuit at Dunedin, and further events at Timaru and Whenuapai. Furthermore at each of these events Bill and II were entered in three different races and the results demonstrated a consistently high score-rate – mostly of wins.

Bill returned to New Zealand in 1989 when Hanuman II was again victorious in the Dunedin road race. The meeting at Wigram followed, providing what Allan Bramwell called "a great day's racing until the last lap of the final race of the day". Bill and James Clark in a Cooper-Bristol collided fifty yards from the finish with fatal consequences for Clark. Bill was a pall-bearer at his funeral and subsequently commissioned the James Clark Memorial Trophy described by Allan Bramwell's daughter, Sue, as a "beautifully made trophy which the Clark family were incredibly touched by".

Racing experiences 3: Thailand and the Bangkok Grand Prix, 1987/8

One of the major events for historic racing cars in the 1980s was the Bangkok Grand Prix, which took place in January 1988. The story of this unique event was recounted in an excellent film *Romulus Returns to Siam*, originally produced in VHF format and then re-issued as a DVD in 2008, as well as in various magazine articles.

The aim of the principal organiser, Narisa Chakrabongse, Prince Chula's daughter and Prince Bira's niece, was to bring to fruition an

Bill's official letter inviting him to race in Thailand in 1987/8.

No. MOD 0400/

August B.E. 2530 (1987)

Dear Mr. Morris,

    Fifty years ago, H.H. Prince Bira, under the patronage of H.R.H. Prince Chula Chakrabongse, was bringing the name of 'Siam', as Thailand was then known, to the attention of the world with his outstanding success in motor racing. As a result in December 1937 the government asked Prince Chula to bring the E.R.A. racing car 'Romulus' to Siam to show to the Thai people. Thus on December 5, 1937 an exciting demonstration run was made along Ratchadamnoern Avenue in Bangkok. On that very day the present King of Thailand, then a young prince, was celebrating his tenth birthday, although no one then imagined the importance that day would later have for the Thai people as the birthday of their beloved King. Now fifty years later this December 5 will be both fifty years since Romulus first came to Thailand and more importantly the 60 th birthday of His Majesty King Bhumibol Adulyadaej.

    In order to commemorate these two anniversaries it was thought that it would be most appropriate if an historic race could be organized. Furthermore as both Prince Chula and Prince Bira were in the Royal Guards regiment and both their fathers were Generals in the service of their country, it is fitting

Before Bangkok: Narisa Chakrabongse and Romulus at Donington, September 1987. Narisa competed at this VSCC meeting to gain experience prior to the Bangkok expedition a few months later. Left to right: Alistair Jarvies, Narisa and Bill.

- 2 -

that the Royal Thai Army should be the main organisers of this event, which will in effect be the Bangkok Grand Prix planned for 1939 but cancelled because of the war.

As the owner of the E.R.A. Hanuman which was one of the cars raced by Prince Bira and contemporary with 'Romulus', the Committee responsible for the 1988 Bira Historic Grand Prix has much pleasure in inviting you and your car to participate in the '1988 Bira Historic Grand Prix' and associated events in January 1988. The Committee hopes that you will honour us with your presence at this event which will not only celebrate the King's birthday and the memory of Prince Bira and Prince Chula, but will also be a symbol of the continuing friendship and goodwill between our two countries.

On behalf of the Committee responsible for the '1988 Bira Historic Grand Prix,' may I say how very much I look forward to seeing you in January 1988.

Yours Sincerely,

(Chavalit Yongchaiyudh)
General, Royal Thai Army
Commander - in - Chief

Mr. W.R.G. Morris
Lower End
Leafield, Oxford, England

Romulus arriving in Thailand on the 18th November 1987, an official welcome for this revered car from Narisa and her co-promoter Sarnpasiri Viriyasiri. All 16 cars and their crews were flown in by Thai International, a major sponsor of the event, along with Shell Thailand Ltd and Montien Hotels. All the cars were then sponsored individually by Thai companies. R12B was appropriately sponsored by Singha Beer to Bill's great enjoyment.

List of cars and competitors Bangkok GP 1988

1. Alfa Romeo P3 – R. Felton
2. ERA 'Remus' – L. Lindsay
3. ERA R12B 'Hanuman' – W.R.G. Morris
4. Bugatti T51 – Sir J. Venables-Llewellyn
5. Bugatti T35B – J. Fitzpatrick
6. MG K3 – P. Bradey
7. BMW 328 – J. Ould
8. Maserati 8C – P. Giddings
9. ERA Delage – A. Mayman, (A.K.Stephens)
10. MG KN/K3 – R. Sweet
11. Bugatti T51A – M. Lane
12. Bugatti T35C – Dr. S. Saunders
13. MG TB Spec – L. Molina
14. Bugatti T39 – A. Valdez

ERA R2B 'Romulus' – M.R. Narisa Chakrabongse

The British Embassy Reception held for the drivers and their teams on January 8, all the cars were arrayed in front of the Embassy.

Narisa demonstrating Romulus up and down Rajdamnern Avenue before the Sprint began.

Scenes from Bangkok:

Clockwise from top left: commemorative plaque for the sprint down Rajdamnern Avenue – the statement of a precise time may be optimistic; at the Sprint are (from left to right) Roger Sweet, Lou Molina, Bill and Ben Morris; Bill in R12B rounding the Democracy Monument in the centre of Bangkok, during his Sprint run.

Romulus, Hanuman and Remus together in the garden at Chakrabongse House

Clockwise from top left:

Bill signing autographs whilst in Thailand in January 1988. The cars were conveyed on very large Thai Army transporters. Bill is on the one carrying 3011, the Maserati 8CM owned and raced by Chula/Bira between 1936 and 1948. ERA R2B Romulus, which was the centre of the celebrations during the expedition to Thailand, is on the right of the picture;

Bill, still innovating in the headwear department;

Leading members of the British contingent display their various trophies: from left to right are Roger Sweet, Bill, Rodney Felton, Ludovic Lindsay, and John Venables-Llewelyn with Narisa in front of the podium;

Bill with the winner's laurels after his victory in Pattaya;

Bill experiencing difficulty with his champagne cork after winning the second circuit race. Narisa is seen in racing overalls, she drove three laps of the circuit in Romulus, ably demonstrating the car, which was not raced.

Bill's invitation to Narisa's White Mouse Ball held on 9 January 1988 between the two main speed events – the sprint down Rajdamnern Way and the circuit racing at Pattaya. Note the request to the ladies to wear appropriately-coloured dresses.

Victoria Morris' response to the dress request (top right) beside a blue and yellow table and an ice-sculpted white mouse. "Several of us took dress patterns over to Thailand and in the preceding week, had them made up in beautiful Thai silks by the Bangkok tailors. I also had a pair of blue and yellow snakeskin shoes made to match along with a silk evening bag. Bill and Ben Morris had 'White Mouse' bow ties made with blue and yellow silk cummerbunds to wear with their evening suits."

R12B Hanuman II, Bill, Victoria (above) with an incarnation of Hanuman in the cockpit. Note Romulus in the background and Ludovic Lindsay in a blue and yellow blazer.

event her father had planned but which never took place. Bira and Chula had returned to Thailand at the end of the 1937 season with Romulus, a visit that aroused great interest. Romulus had been demonstrated along one of Bangkok's principal streets and had been on display. Chula planned to take things a stage further in 1939 and bring to Thailand a collection of cars and drivers: in effect to stage a European motor race in an Asian context. Plans were quite well advanced, but the War put paid to the project and in the immediate post-war years conditions in both countries made it a non-starter.

Bill played a leading part in the Thailand expedition. He had rehabilitated Romulus in the mid-1970s (fully described in chapter 5) the car that was to be at the centre of the event, he was taking II, an authentic ex-Bira car, to drive himself and he provided much advice and practical help to Narisa when she was planning the whole event.

The competitive side of the expedition took two main forms with a sprint down Rajdamnern Avenue in the centre of Bangkok and a circuit event at Pattaya. Bira had driven Romulus down Rajdamnern Avenue in 1937 so there were some strong historical echoes for the first part of the proceedings. One of the most amusing parts of the film *Romulus Returns to Siam* was Bill being briefed by John Ure (of whom more later in this chapter) as they drive down Rajdamnern Avenue in one of the Thai taxis, which looks rather like a large basket on wheels powered by a motor cycle engine. As the driver weaved through the traffic, Bill clearly found the experience rather terrifying; driving Hanuman II, by comparison, would be a relatively safe and sedate experience. The route the sprint followed incorporated a rather prominent bump which pre-war suspensions found rather demanding. Hanuman II was not on his best form and Rodney Felton, driving his P3 Alfa, looked to be the fastest of the British contingent.

A week later the whole entourage of cars and drivers moved 100 kilometres south west to Pattaya for a circuit event. Tony Stephens described this track as a "a mixture of Oulton Park and Cadwell Park with a lot of concrete barriers"; Alain de Cadenet, who was acting as mechanic for the ex-Bira 8CM Maserati, thought it was a mixture of Oulton Park and Donington: there is a common thread somewhere! Prior to the racing Narisa completed three demonstration laps with Romulus following a similar demonstration run up and down Rajdamnern Avenue before the sprint.

There were two races of ten laps each and the outcome seemed to satisfy almost everyone. Rodney Felton's Alfa was again the fastest car and he won the

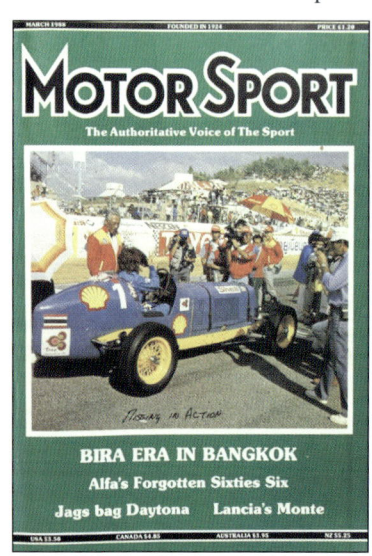

The Bob Gerard Trophy, one of the ERA Club's main awards, was won by Bill in 1987 and by Narisa in 1988. Here is Bill presenting the trophy to Narisa in recognition of her organisation of the Bangkok expedition.

first race relatively easily with Bill, Ludovic Lindsay in R5B *Remus* and Roger Sweet in his twin o.h.c. MG as his nearest rivals. Rodney also emerged as the overall winner, but the second race was much more competitive. Bill kept hard on Rodney's heels throughout the race and when the Alfa went a little wide on the penultimate lap Bill grabbed his opportunity and went into the lead. He took the chequered flag to the delight of the Thai spectators. The perspiring drivers (it was clearly very, very hot) celebrated with some champagne, and anything else they could lay their hands on to cool down.

Understandably this whole expedition had a big impact on all those who took part. Quite apart from the actual racing there was plenty of opportunity for sightseeing as well as a good deal of social activity. Narisa organised a spectacular ball at her riverside mansion, which took place in the interval between the two main competitive events. At this ball the legend of Hanuman was enacted by a group of Thai dancers. As Tony Stephens described it: "The dancing Hanuman was introduced on the floor to the rather embarrassed driver of the eponymous car, to the great delight of the other guests". This particular incident is not included in the film, so sparing Bill's blushes!

Hanuman II – rebuilding the car, taking on new 'pilots' and thinking about selling

As we've seen in the previous chapter, right from the start with Hanuman II Bill was his own chief mechanic and that remained the position for his whole career. The major rebuild of R12B in 1965 taught him a considerable amount about the basic features of ERA design and that knowledge was further enhanced once the decision to reconstruct

R12C was taken (discussed in Chapter Four). Bill's identity as both chief mechanic and driver was vividly illustrated in an incident during the second Monaco historic meeting in 1982. Hanuman II's throttle linkage was giving trouble so Bill stopped on the circuit by a fire crew, borrowed a pair of pliers from one of its attendants, and made a hasty repair. He cranked the engine back into life with the starting handle and sped off to complete the race!

Three years after this Monaco incident Hanuman II's second major rebuild was underway and, as already indicated, this time Bill's main strategic objective was to lighten the car. Prior to embarking on that rebuild, Bill had decided to sell R12B and it had been advertised in *Motor Sport* in June 1984 complete with extensive spares and the car's transporter. Bill had been offered the opportunity to buy an 8CTF Maserati from Cameron Millar and this had considerable appeal as a new challenge after more than twenty years with Hanuman II; Bill would still have retained an ERA interest with R12C, which was currently on loan to Tony Stephens. Unfortunately Bill was not able to synchronise the sale and purchase of the two cars so the projected deal fell through.

Hanuman II's third major rebuild took place in 1993/4 and unlike the previous two it was a matter of necessity not of choice, as it had been damaged in the crash in New Zealand at the beginning of 1989. This crash greatly upset Bill and for some years he could not contemplate sorting out the damage and returning R12B to competition. In fact it was Duncan Ricketts who eventually undertook the work. Ricketts had emerged as a leading ERA driver as well as a highly-skilled ERA preparer and we shall encounter him again in yet another identity in the following chapter as the creator of R12C's new body. Duncan had been racing R1B since 1987 for Patrick Marsh's widow, Sally, and had become a close friend of Bill (who had originally recommended him to Sally to take over the driving and maintenance of Patrick's ERA). Duncan had learnt a good deal from Bill about the dynamics (and occasionally the statics!) of ERAs.

Duncan knew about Bill's problems with R12B so he suggested that he should take over the rebuild and then compete with it in 1994. That would allow him to give R1B a much needed basic overhaul and avoid having to drop out of racing for a season. As it turned out R1B didn't receive its 'chassis-up' restoration as there was a lot of pressure to keep the car active during ERA's diamond jubilee year.

The rebuild of Hanuman II was a major undertaking. The chassis was 'banana shaped' on both sides, there was some damage to the engine, the radiator was bent, as were some of the body panels and the fuel tank had been damaged. Duncan made an interesting discovery about the chassis,

R12B Hanuman II returns to racing in 1994. Duncan Ricketts is warming-up R12B's engine at the April 1994 VSCC meeting. Bill is on the left just behind the car, Tony Stephens on the right and Ben Morris to the right of Bill. Duncan finished third in the Patrick Lindsay Trophy Race. Later in the season Duncan and Hanuman II won the Bob Gerard Trophy Race at Mallory Park.

In this picture (left) they are on the tail of John Harper in R4D.

Duncan in typically determined mood. (below)

namely that one side was a quarter of an inch longer than the other. When this was reported to Bill he said: "It might explain why it was always better round right hand bends than left ones!" It led Duncan to wonder whether the whole of R8B's chassis had been used by the White Mouse Garage in the post-Reims reconstruction. Another possibility is that when the Chula équipe acquired R8B's chassis it was already in its unequal form due to earlier damage. In May 1937 Earl Howe had a serious accident at Brooklands. Repairs carried out at that time might have involved replacing one of the rails, or straightening the existing ones in such a manner that the two did not emerge exactly equal.

At any rate, whatever the explanation, Duncan equalised the chassis rails and all the other repair and reconstruction work was completed for the beginning of the 1994 racing season. Bill now acted as entrant with Duncan driving in four British events and John Ure in three before it was 'exported' to Australia for some more racing. The car went almost faultlessly and produced a string of good results. Duncan found Hanuman II "very different" from R1B. The latter car was "powerful but heavy, most of the suspension parts were worn, not badly, but enough to give a general loose feeling. R12B Hanuman II, by contrast was a light and nimble car, it seemed much easier to drive, and the only slightly disappointing part was the brakes. Being hydraulic they didn't quite have the feel of R1B's". As he became more familiar with R12B it "seemed to get better and better". The year turned out to be a very good one for Duncan with some outstanding results with both ERAs: "Just as I had pulled out all the stops with R12B and won a race, the next outing with R1B would seem to go even better, both cars just appeared to go quicker and quicker. It seemed to be one of those memorable years when everything went right."

Other 'pilots' for Hanuman II: Ben Morris, Phil Hill, John Ure and Tony Stephens

Nearly twenty years before Duncan was in Hanuman II's driving seat, Bill's brother had occupied it on a number of occasions during 1976, a year in which Bill was busy with the revived Romulus. Although Ben had had some rallying experiences he hadn't previously circuit-raced and his Hanuman II 'training' consisted of an hour or two's practice on the Friday afternoon immediately before the first VSCC Silverstone meeting of 1976! On race-day he acquitted himself sufficiently well to be awarded the Driver of the Day award which brought him £25 – very welcome to his supporters who spent most of it celebrating in the pub! Ben had the interesting experience of taking the car to Donington for the 1961 World Champion, Phil Hill. Ben found Hill a very pleasant and sympathetic person and subsequently he sent Ben a personal signed photograph expressing his thanks.

Hill was test-driving the car for a feature in the American magazine *Road and Track* in the course of which he said: "Of all the cars I would be driving… this is the one I was looking forward to the most. The ERA is a delightfully responsive car right from the first turn of the wheel as it has been developed to be a torquey car. I had a ball driving it. In my opinion this car gives you more of a feeling of what this whole era was about: it's just a damned honest vehicle. Actually this car is much more than I thought it would be, having read about them as a boy. You can feel there was some real devoted individual development and that the drivers were in on the whole thing. When the ERA drive was over, I can say that I was not in the least disappointed. The dreamy romantic feeling I held of English racing when I was a schoolboy was totally recaptured by driving this car and it sort of justified all my original feelings about automobiles and racing."

John Ure, who became a leading driver of ERAs during the 1990s, served his mechanical and driving apprenticeship with Bill. He first made contact with the White Mouse équipe at the Monaco meeting in 1979 to which Bill had taken Romulus (described in chapter 5). John had hitched down and slept on the beach despite the authorities' attempts to move him on, as they were not very sympathetic to impecunious racing enthusiasts! He learnt a lot over the next few years working on R12B and in September 1988 had his first ERA drive at Oulton Park in the car. It was a memorable experience for a number of reasons.

A fine action shot of John Ure in his first race with R12B – at the AMOC Oulton Park meeting in September 1988. It was not the most comfortable of drives as the rear seat cushion was taken out to accommodate John's long legs. For all that, he finished fifth, a very creditable result for his debut in the car.

R12B had been racing at Donington the previous day and needed a gearbox change. At this time the five speed box was being used but the spare was a conventional four speed version and John had to remember what this meant for the gear-change mechanism. John is a tall man with long legs and to help him fit into Hanuman's cockpit the back seat cushion was removed. Not surprisingly he found it a "bloody uncomfortable" experience but he finished a respectable fifth and with the gearbox intact!

Another of R12B's pilots who began as a helper was Tony Stephens, whom we shall encounter again in the next chapter. As that chapter recounts, Tony's first competitive ERA experience was with R12C, but in 1995 Bill decided to swap that car with Hanuman II. Tony therefore returned R12C to Bill and was loaned Hanuman II which he raced for the next three and a half seasons. Although Tony had been familiar with the car since the mid-1970s it was as a helper and he had never raced it. When he did start driving it he found it a 'revelation' and his results showed a marked improvement on what he had been able to achieve with R12C. Unlike Bill, Tony is keen on the hills and he was able to turn in times at venues such as Prescott and Loton Park which were among the very best and fully competitive with the fastest two-litre ERAs.

Bill finally decided to sell Hanuman II during the winter of 1998/9. Initially as a co-owner, then from 1974 as the sole owner he had had thirty-seven years of continuous association with the car. Obviously

Tony Stephens holding a 4CM Maserati at bay

> # ERA CHASSIS No R12B
> ## Ex Prince Bira Hanuman II
>
> 1½-litre supercharged car in original Bira trim and colours. Highly successful, ready to race, and very well known. Many new and secondhand spares, present owner 22 years.
> **1974 Mercedes 408 Van / Transporter** complete with ramps and winch, MoT £800.
> **1971 Ferrari Dino 246.** Red, in excellent order, complete service history confirms mileage of 63,000 miles, MoT and tax. £6,750
> **1930 Ford Model A pick-up.** in Excellent original order, yellow and black, no current MoT or tax. £2,500.
> **Exciting new project reason for sale.**
>
> ### Bill Morris, Lower End, Leafield, Oxon.
> ### Asthall Leigh 687

Bill's advert for R12B in June 1984 Motor Sport.

there were some regrets after such a long period but as we have seen he had considered selling it on at least two occasions before. By the time he came to sell ERAs had become a valuable 'commodity', certainly worth a great deal more than the £750 that had been paid for Hanuman II in 1962, whatever adjustment is made for inflation. Bill's attitude to this very big increase in their value was that it didn't change in any way the basic point of owning a racing car which was to race it, not to put it into a museum or least of all in a heated store room. Equally he wasn't indifferent to their enhanced value and Hanuman II's disposal price reflected the market rate together with his substantial investment, both of time and money, over nearly forty years. A well-known and successful car was unlikely to linger long on the market and in March 1999 it passed to David Wenman.

Chapter Four

R12C recreated – from the 1960s to the 1990s

The task ahead

When Bill and David bought R12B, they knew little about its history. Neither had read the various books that Chula and Bira had written about their racing experiences in the 1930s. However, they soon caught up with the historical background and worked out where their unexpected spare chassis fitted into the story. Both were attracted by the idea of reconstructing R12C and early in their ownership they committed themselves to carrying it through. Nevertheless they were fully aware that they faced some real and substantial problems.

Finding the i.f.s.

The most serious of these difficulties was the absence of any independent front suspension (i.f.s.) If R12C was to be faithful to its C type identity it had to have i.f.s. As we have already seen, the major reason for rebuilding R12C after the 1939 accident on R8B's chassis was the absence of any spare i.f.s. Bill and David needed a proverbial Fairy Godmother and it was Jim Berry's widow, Vera, who fitted this role completely.

Jim had been killed testing the JBW-Maserati at Oulton Park in April 1962. He had been a mainstay of the hill climb and sprint scene throughout the 1950s driving a variety of cars. In 1959 he had bought R4D from Tom Norton, who in turn had taken over the ex-Mays ERA after Ken Wharton had been killed in New Zealand at the beginning of 1957. After Jim's death Mrs Berry gradually sold off his competition cars.

By the time Bill and David went to see her, R4D had already been sold to Peter Brewer. On their first visit they found a considerable number of ERA parts but it was on a subsequent visit that Bill found what they really needed. Foraging around in the loft where Jim had accumulated various spares, he uncovered two tea chests, each of which bore the initials 'RM' on the outside. These chests contained a brand new set of independent front suspension parts complete with brakes. What he had found was the spare set for R4D; 'RM', of course, stood for Raymond Mays. As Bill said: "Christmas had arrived in a big way": not only was this the single most vital component needed for the rebuild but it came at no cost. Vera Berry would not accept any payment despite being pressed to do so: "No, no, Jim would have helped any youngsters with their cars. You can have them – I'm pleased you have found what you wanted".

There was an interesting footnote to this providential visit. Shortly after Bill had taken the suspension parts back to Lancaster Mews, Peter Brewer came down from Macclesfield having discovered that he had missed R4D's spare suspension. Given its importance in the reconstruction of R12C Bill and David were not in a negotiating mood!

Reviving the Chula/Bira connection

The visit to Mrs Berry was one of a large number that Bill and David undertook once the historical significance of both R12B and R12C was appreciated. The aim was to fill in the background to the cars and collect up sufficient parts to make the reconstruction a viable project. Prince Chula had died in December 1963 and neither Bill nor David ever met him. However they did make contact with his widow, Princess Chula, and David went down to their large house, Tredethy, near Bodmin where Chula had been living since the end of the war. Quite apart from Romulus himself, which Chula had retained in a private museum since the Bira/Chula stable broke up, there were a number of other cars and bits of equipment that had survived from the pre-war years. Princess Chula provided one or two important components. One was a fuel tank which had been a spare for Romulus: this was subsequently swapped for one that Sandy Murray had which was more suitable for a C type car, with the Romulus spare suiting Murray's R1A. Princess Chula also gave them a radiator cowl, which had been on R12C at the time of the Reims crash and it still bore the damage then inflicted, together with a spare block with a large hole in it (subsequently repaired).

Bill met Shura Rahm and Stanley Holgate, both of whom had played major roles in the Chula/Bira équipe. They clarified the basis on which R12B Hanuman II had been rebuilt, after the Reims crash, but by the mid-1960s neither retained any substantial stock of ERA parts. Bill did buy from Rahm a set of Ulysse Nardin chronometers which he believed were only one of three sets: Rahm himself and the Chakrabongse family had one set each and the third set was owned by A.V. Ebblewhite, the famous Brooklands time-keeper. In fact most of the White Mouse Stable's stock of spare parts had been bought by Bob Gerard in 1949. Bob's Leicester headquarters were visited but, according to David, most

Reconstruction of R12C! The search for parts.

The letter sent by Bill to Princess Chula is dated November 1966 ...

> 4 Beech Walk,
> Grove Park,
> TRING,
> Herts.
>
> 21st November, 1966.
>
> Madam,
>
> I do hope that you will not mind me writing this letter to you but being the joint owner of one of the E.R.A.'s which used to belong to your late husband, Prince Chula, I trust that you may obtain a certain amount of amusement and interest from it.
>
> David Kergon and myself own Hanuman II and since we carried out an 18 month re-build of the car, (see pages 36 and 37 of the enclosed 'Sporting Motorist' magazine), we have had some very enjoyable times with the car and it is now going so well that we have become Runners Up in The Historic Racing Car Trophy and the E.R.A. Trophy, annual awards presented by The Vintage Sports Car Club.
>
> When we purchased Hanuman II from South Africa over 4 years ago we were sent with the car the chassis and several other components from the original Hanuman, which was crashed by Prince Bira at Rheims in 1939. During the re-build of Hanuman II we have managed to collect enough parts to enable a build-up of the original Hanuman to be contemplated, especially as we have now obtained the main part that was missing i.e the independent front suspension units.
>
> However, we are still short of several important components and here we come to the reason for this letter to you; I know you still keep at Bodmin some parts from the cars and we write in the hope that you may be able to perhaps let us have them in order to bring Hanuman back to the circuits again.
>
> The parts we are very anxious to have are the tail section from Romulus, which was taken off and replaced by the larger capacity tank and which is still on the car, which is now on show at the Montagu Motor Museum; the Brooklands Exhaust Pipe and the Nose Cowl from the crashed Hanuman, however badly bent it may be.
>
> Cont'd.........

of what was on offer by the mid-1960s, was both rather worn and quite expensive. However, they did find an inlet manifold which was stamped with R12C's original engine number (5013), so this was purchased.

Getting it together: the main sources for R12C's rebuild

There were four main sources for R12C's rebuild. First and foremost, there was the original chassis, secondly various genuine ERA spares were used, some of which had been part of R12B Hanuman II or R12C throughout their history; thirdly various newly manufactured parts were commissioned; and finally there were a few elements which were non-ERA in origin but adapted for R12C's use. It is worth saying a little more about each of these broad categories.

> Please forgive our impertinence for writing to you but we are anxious to keep the car as original as possible and if we cannot obtain these parts then we will have to make them ourselves, or where impracticable, have them made outside and these will then become replica parts, i.e. non-original.
>
> We find it difficult to know what to offer you in exchange for these valuable parts, even if you are prepared to let them go, but we could offer you the amount of money it would cost to have the replica parts made, but money seems so impersonal and as a result we were wondering whether you would care to accept the offer of a scale model in die-cast metal of Hanuman II that we have recently completed. It is about 6" long and painted in the correct blue and yellow colours and is in fact a direct copy of Hanuman II in it's present state, which is as re-built in 1940 by Stan Holgate.
>
> We also enclose a recent copy of 'Autosport' in which you will find a report from that famous Motor Racing Personality, John Bolster, when he tried Hanuman II at Brands Hatch recently. He certainly enjoyed himself on that day as it was the first time he had driven such a car since his unfortunate accident in the British Grand Prix in the late 1940's.
>
> You will be pleased to hear that both Remus and Hanuman II have a tremendous following in Vintage and Historic car events in this country and also abroad and that they are still running as well as ever before. It is indeed a pity that Romulus isn't running with us but it's marvellous to see it having pride of place at Lord Montagu's Museum.
>
> We do hope you will seriously consider our offer and we would be delighted to come and discuss the matter personally with you if so desired. Romulus, Remus and Hanuman II have provided us with a tremendous amount of entertainment and enjoyment and have done ever since we saw Remus when still schoolboys, and we are now striving to complete the quartet of all Prince Chula's E.R.A.'s.
>
> Yours sincerely,
>
> W. R. G. Morris

(i) The chassis

There are other cases of racing car chassis which have been abandoned at some stage and lain unused for many years only eventually to be revived in some form. The case of R12C must surely rate as one of the most remarkable: damaged and discarded in 1939, passing though the hands of six different owners before Bill and David acquired it twenty-three years later, after a journey to and from Africa. It is interesting, and slightly odd, that the late Denis Jenkinson, usually a stickler for historical accuracy, always seemed reluctant to acknowledge that R12C's reconstruction was on its original 1937 chassis. As we detail below, a lot of spare parts and replacement parts *were* used, but for most people the chassis is of fundamental importance in establishing a car's provenance.

The 1939 accident had damaged the chassis but not in a very serious manner. It was kinked at the front end round the suspension mountings and it was sent to Rubery Owen in Acton to be straightened out. It had to be slightly adapted subsequently to accommodate the D type i.f.s., which has shorter arms than the system produced for the C type cars. A tube had

... and the following month the Princess' secretary responded, confirming that she had two of the three parts Bill and David were seeking, namely a tail section and a nose cowl.

> TREDETHY
> BODMIN
> CORNWALL
> TELEPHONE ST MABYN 232
>
> 6th December, 1966.
>
> Dear Mr. Morris,
>
> I have been asked by Princess Chula, who is very busy preparing for her departure for Thailand at the end of this month, to reply to your letter of 21st November.
>
> The Princess was very pleased to hear all the news of Remus and Hanuman II, and was most interested to read the articles in the magazines you enclosed.
>
> We do, in fact, have the tail section and the nose cowl that you require, but the only exhaust pipe we have is, I believe, off a Delage - I may be wrong. However, the Princess is quite willing to let you have these parts, and she would be delighted to have the scale model of Hanuman II in exchange.
>
> Perhaps you will kindly let me know direct when you would like to come and collect these parts, and at the same time the Princess has suggested that you might care to have a look at her motor-racing trophy room.
>
> Yours sincerely,
>
> Major R.W. Potts.
> Private Secretary.
>
> W.R.G. Morris, Esq.,
> 4, Beech Walk,
> Grove Park,
> Tring,
> Herts.

to be welded across the front end and this later work was carried out by Brian Hall, a metal fettler who lived in the next village to Bill at Leafield.

(ii) Spare parts

So far as ERA spares were concerned, we have already noted some examples including the single most vital element, the i.f.s. that came from R4D. Apart from contacting individuals such as Bob Gerard or Stan Holgate, it was a case of keeping one's eyes open for suitable opportunities. Bill made a number of sorties in response to adverts or information about likely sources. Some back brake parts were taken off a special in Hull in the late 1960s and a year or two before this he had bought the ex-Jim Berry Cooper-ERA. Its chief attraction was its ERA gearbox, originally a spare for R4D. Bill was only interested in the gearbox and once he had removed it the rest of the car was sold on to Dick Crosthwaite for a Cooper-Bristol re-creation.

Bill managed to contact a large number of people who had had ERA connections and he covered many miles driving round the country in pursuit of parts, from single valves to complete radiators. He met "some very odd characters and some very wonderful characters" and found it amazing what had been "borrowed" from the factory, often from the earliest days of ERA, so that some of the parts had been lying around for the best part of thirty years.

One of the components Bill chased after gave rise to one of the best-known bits of ERA folklore. In 1966 Bill saw an advert for an ERA rev counter and set off on the long journey to Cumbria. When he got there he was directed to the "wreck of a special" under a tarpaulin in the garden where he disconnected the rev counter. After he had paid the agreed price of £10, he set off back to London, but hadn't gone very far before he felt rather weary. He pulled off into a lay-by and dozed off but was woken by the sound of something "scorching past my bonnet". He recognized it was Gordon Chapman in his DB5 Aston Martin. Bill thought "Poor chap, he's missed the rev counter". When he subsequently spoke to Gordon he expressed sympathy for his wasted trip. "Oh no, it wasn't that at all", said Gordon. "Well I've got the rev counter here, I'm very pleased with it" said Bill, now somewhat puzzled. "Oh yes, pity about that", Gordon responded "But you missed the car". "What car?" said Bill. "You missed GP2, the E type ERA!"

Gordon had spotted that under a misleading Williams and Pritchard coupe body the basis for the 'special' was the second E type ERA. He already owned GP1 which he had acquired from Jim Berry in 1959. As Chapter Six recounts, many years later it was Bill who drove GP2 for Gordon when it had been restored to its proper ERA form. Not surprisingly Bill and Gordon 'dined out' on this tale for many years after and it has been widely appreciated by others.

The engine for R12C was the one previously used in Hanuman II, number 5013. This necessitated building up a new engine for R12B which Bill did by using the cylinder block from Princess Chula and the many spare parts that came with the car and the chassis from Southern Rhodesia. R12C's engine incorporates distinctive C type connecting rods which have four bolts; these were also in the spares that originally accompanied the car.

The driving seat for the car came from R8C, via John Vessey, a well known competitor in VSCC circles. When Cuth Harrison re-bodied R8C in the early post-war years he used a conventional bucket seat, thus making the original ERA 'armchair' version redundant. Another significant modification, the conversion of R11B to wet sump lubrication, provided an oil tank for R12C.

(iii) New parts

The third category of specially manufactured parts involved most of the body and certain mechanical components such as the crankshaft, rear axle, torque tubes and the propeller shaft. By the time the car was ready for its body it had passed into the care of Tony Stephens. Tony had asked one of the reputable panel beating firms what it would cost to 'clothe' R12C. Not wholly to his surprise, he found it was "quite a lot and certainly far more than I could afford". When Tony was re-telling this in his local hostelry, the landlord said that he ought to speak to Lawrie Kimber who would almost certainly know someone who could assist Tony. This was the cue for Duncan Ricketts: after an apprenticeship in the prototype department at what was then British Leyland's Cowley works, Duncan had gone to work for Lawrie Kimber. Duncan and Tony were introduced to each other in the Green Dragon and a deal was struck. Tony thinks that what was interesting about this initial contact was that both were not being exactly straightforward: "Duncan wasn't going to tell me that he had not worked in aluminium before and I wasn't going to tell him that I

Three shots of R12C Hanuman taken as Tony Stephens was building up the car in his workshop in Haddenham.

The first (above left) shows the engine end of the Godfrey blower and the two carburettors: the supercharger manifold is not yet complete.

Next (above right) is the cockpit with instruments in place.

And this picture (left) shows the i.f.s and other features of the front end. The cat seen descending from the cockpit used to curl up in the seat, a testament to the armchair comfort of the ERA driver's seat!

didn't trust him to do the job until I had seen a bit!" Their initial agreement was that Duncan should make a scuttle for R12C, using Hanuman II's to copy from as it was temporarily detached from the rest of the car.

Duncan's previous experience of vintage work was confined to making a few panels for MGs. He *had* seen ERA R1B competing the previous year at Brands Hatch – a remarkable coincidence as more than ten years later it was the car with which he began his ERA driving career when he was entered by Sally Marsh after the sadly premature death of her husband Patrick Marsh.

His initiation into the complexities of making an ERA body was a severely practical one: "Tony arrived with the scuttle and left. A week later I had copied it and he took it away and fitted it to the car. He returned with two noses, an original one that was quite badly damaged

A photograph taken by David Weguelin, while compiling his definitive book on ERA history outside Tony's workshop, both Tony and Bill looking relaxed and happy. The new scuttle was made by Duncan Ricketts 'on approval'!

and another one to copy the general shape for R12C. I didn't have any photographs or drawings to work from". The damaged nose was the one Princess Chula had given Bill and David and it proved possible to restore it so that it could be fitted to R12C.

The whole process went amazingly smoothly considering Duncan's lack of experience and the very limited information he had to work from. He recollects "having a few problems with making louvres but they turned out well". His main difficulty was "not having the welding experience and not having the patterns to make the panels over. When I made bodies at British Leyland we always had wooden moulds to work with, very experienced craftsman to get help from and we never worked with aluminium". Nevertheless the end product was of a very high standard and, not surprisingly, Duncan has been making ERA bodywork ever since.

(iv) Adapted parts

The final source of R12C's rebuild was various mechanical components which had no connection with ERA in origin but lent themselves to suitable adaptation. Thus some Land Rover wheel rims were used for the front and back wheels which were spoked to original ERA hubs. The Land Rover also supplied a steering idler box. David Brown was the source of track rods, track rod ends and the drag link, but these did not come from an Aston Martin but from the more humble tractors produced by the firm!

Purists might find this final category not wholly to their liking but as Bill emphasised, when the restoration of R12C was first planned and set in hand, they simply did not have the resources to ensure that every single component was 'authentic'. Furthermore, a more relaxed mood prevailed at that time – the concern with authenticity for vintage and historic racing cars lay some way in the future.

To Zoller or not to Zoller?

The Zoller blower was, of course, one of the key defining features of the C type ERA and it was therefore hardly surprising that Bill and David's original intention was that R12C should have such a supercharger. However deciding that they wished to install one and actually getting one to work satisfactorily were two entirely different things.

The problems of the Zoller have been noted in Chapter One and with the sole exception of R4D all the ERAs using them had stopped doing so by 1950. Why had they all been discarded? Bill summarises the situation in this way: "A lot of hot air has been pushed around about Zollers over the years, most of it not true, but the one thing that most people agree on is that they are troublesome and that bit is true".

If there was pretty general agreement that Zollers were a headache, there was much more argument about *exactly* what the problem was and how it might be cured. This is where a lot of Bill's 'hot air' comes in, with all kinds of different assertions as to which elements e.g. the vanes, the guides, the casing, the carburettors were at fault. Bill responded to the different diagnoses rectifying various faults but the results were disappointing: "They were no better, not one bloody ounce better".

Bill was not easily deterred and he set up the blowers with an electric motor with the aim of simulating, as far as possible, the circumstances of a real engine. He describes what happened: "very quickly we found that the temperature round the carburettors and their mountings on the blower case was below freezing due to the evaporation of the methanol, whereas the temperature on the outlet pipe was up to 100 degrees centigrade at some stages. Now on the Zoller vane blower used on the ERA, the inlet and outlet ports are next door to each other and this differential in heat was causing the blower case to distort, the vanes to touch the case, and the net result was either a shower of alloy filings in the engine or a seized blower"

Subsequently, Bill had a real-life experience when he tested R4D for Anthony Mayman after Jim Fitzgerald had fitted a steel liner to its Zoller to rub the blades on and stop them distorting. Bill was going round Maggots when he saw a F5000 coming up behind him "so I lifted off and that was the start of my troubles as the blower exploded. I saw

Two views of the supercharger installed in R12C Hanuman for fourteen years, 1982–1995. It was a K300 made by Sir George Godfrey and Partners and as the numbers on the identification plate state, was built in February 1969. Its position in the middle of the cockpit on top of the gearbox was more or less identical to that of the original Zoller. Compare this with the photograph of the Zoller in R12C in Chapter One (see page 16).

the bonnet lift off and all the instruments fell out of the dashboard and I immediately stopped the car. Anthony came up to me later and said he was glad he wasn't driving it at the time!"

As Bill's own experiments weren't moving him any closer to a solution, he decided to use a K300 Roots blower which was made up by Sir George Godfrey and Partners. An adaptor plate was cast to link the Zoller drive take-off assembly with the new Roots type supercharger. The original carburettors and Zoller outlet manifold came from Donald Day, whose ex-Gerard car had played an important part in firing Bill's initial enthusiasm for ERAs.

Passing on the baton…

Progress on the R12C project was dependent on a number of factors. Bill and David were committed to racing Hanuman II and both faced the unavoidable necessity of earning their daily bread, which was becoming more, rather than less, onerous as they made their way up the managerial ladder. Keeping Hanuman II active meant spending time and money on it and inevitably that limited what could be done on R12C. When Brian Jordan visited Lancaster Mews at the end of 1965 the hope was that R12C would be completed within five years. A certain amount of progress had been made by the early-mid 1970s but it was still a long way from being finished.

A number of things then happened which changed matters quite substantially. As already related in the previous chapter, David Kergon bowed out of his racing partnership with Bill at the end of 1974. Bill therefore had sole responsibility for both R12B and R12C. In 1975 Smiths Industries sent Bill out to South Africa for a spell and when he arrived back he found not two but three ERAs in his garage at Leafield! As the next chapter recounts, this third ERA was Romulus (R2B) which Prince and Princess Chula's daughter, Narisa Chakrabongse, had inherited following her mother's death in 1971. She had decided that it needed a thorough overhaul and that Bill was the man for the job. Accordingly, Romulus had been taken to Leafield complete with his electrical heater which enabled Bill to explain why his tenant had been complaining about excessive electricity bills!

Bill thought that two ERAs in the garage was bad enough, but three was quite impossible. He therefore decided to loan R12C to Tony Stephens. Tony had been helping Bill with R12B for some time and was very happy to pick up the challenge of finishing off what Bill had begun. When the car left Leafield to go to Tony's base it was on four wheels with an engine and a gearbox, a fuel tank and a blower, which was coupled up but without carburettors.

Completing the reconstruction

Tony had two main tasks – to supply a large number of small fittings and to create a functioning racing car from all the assembled components. The component that caused the most difficulty was the steering box. There were no original drawings available and no spares forthcoming from other owners. Tony made some castings by borrowing Romulus' box when it was being overhauled. The kernel of the problem was the worm, which had to operate in the opposite direction to that in the A and B type cars. Tony was told, by a senior engineer at GKN, that it should be fashioned from phosphor bronze. GKN was occasionally commissioned to do work in such material and after one such job, offered a small amount of the surplus to Tony. He then had to get the right thread cut. Despite contacting every gear cutting firm south of the Wash, Tony could not find one with the right equipment to do the job. Eventually Bill came up with the solution as a by-product of selling a number of superchargers to Barry Linger. When Bill asked Barry what line of country he was in, Barry said he had recently set up on his own to carry out gear cutting work. "Ah", said Bill, "Then I've got a job that you might be able to tackle but it needs a very special kind of machine". "Yes, that's no problem" he replied, "I've got one of those!"

Firing it up: R12C runs under its own steam

After making all the necessary parts and then connecting everything together, and some of the processes such as the manifolding for the supercharger took a lot of time, Tony completed the car in early 1982. He took the car to Bill's at Leafield and it was towed up the village street without fitting the sparking plugs, in order to get some oil pressure. With the plugs refitted, it was then towed in the other direction and it started up immediately. As might be imagined Tony was absolutely delighted to see all his work come to a successful conclusion. The engine was inspected to make sure the oil was circulating and apart from one bit of over-enthusiastic soldering everything was flowing where it was intended.

The next stage was to drive it around – at rather greater speed than allowed for in the village street or in Bill's yard! – and that meant a trip to Little Rissington airfield which lies just off the rather splendid road between Stow-on-the Wold and Burford. When they got it up to Rissington everything seemed to be working well. There was a little experimenting with different needles in order to obtain the right mixture, but no serious problems.

The first firing-up of R12C at Leafield in March 1982.

Tony is being towed by Bill on the outskirts of Leafield, a moment or two later the car fired for the first time since 1939.

The yard at Leafield with the rear wheels spinning on the jack. Bill is checking the engine and Tony is looking at the blower. A quick lift jack has to be used when warming the engine as the gearbox has a rear mounted oil pump which only operates when the transmission is running, i.e. a gear is selected.

Racing experience with R12C

R12C aroused considerable interest on its race debut at the VSCC's Silverstone meeting in April 1982. In characteristic manner Patrick Lindsay came over to examine the car saying to Tony: "Let's see the new ERA". Without more ado he jumped into it exclaiming: "My God, Tony, it's like a tart's boudoir!" Tony asked him to remember "how beautiful it was" when they were out on the racing track. Such a request still allowed Patrick to pass Tony on the *inside* of Woodcote, almost locking wheels in the process!

During the fourteen seasons that Tony drove R12C it proved a reliable racing car: overwhelmingly where it was entered it ran and where it started it usually finished the race. However, Tony did not find it a wholly satisfactory experience with the chief weakness lying in the car's handling. Tony attributes this problem basically to a combination

The first appearance at a race meeting of R12B and R12C together: R12B on the left, R12C on the right. The occasion was the VSCC's Silverstone meeting, April 1982.

The proximity to 'Courage Best Bitter' and 'Hofmeister' was no accident! This was the favoured paddock spot and Bill's collection of beer glasses at home bore testament to the popularity of the nearby bar – it may have been this occasion when Bill and Ben returned to find a flowerpot on the seat of each ERA – Bill and Ben the Flowerpot Men!

This dramatic picture by Harold Barker illustrates the kind of problem Tony Stephens experienced with R12C Hanuman: on this occasion at the original Woodcote corner at Silverstone in June 1986.

R12C at Silverstone in 1982 with Ben Morris looking into the cockpit, Bill on the other side and Tony Stephens enjoying a refresher. Ben Morris and Tony both drove R12C at this VSCC July Silverstone meeting. Bill was out of luck as R12B had cylinder head problems and had to be retired. The photo gives a good view of the Porsche i.f.s.

of a ground level roll centre at the front with a high roll centre at the rear. He doesn't think ERA's decision to adopt the Porsche i.f.s. was a particularly good one especially the short arm version – R4D's spare – which was fitted to R12C. It resulted in a degree of unpredictability and a feeling that the car "was determined to try and kill you at each race but you could never tell which corner it was going to be on!" Tony worked away at this problem, his main innovation being to fit an anti-roll bar, which undoubtedly improved things, but didn't overcome the basic problem of different roll centres.

Other drivers did handle R12C occasionally. Bill himself drove it in the Hawthorn Memorial Trophy race at Silverstone in July 1986. He won the special trophy given for the first pre-war car to finish, as this race is chiefly for post-1945 racing cars. He didn't recall too much about the experience though he *was* struck by the smoothness of the engine: "it didn't have any of the roughness or vibration that I have always associated with R12B's mechanical bits". He thinks this was probably due to the size of the Godfrey supercharger acting as some kind of vibration damper. He didn't recall that the car was especially difficult to handle, but acknowledged his experience was very limited.

John Venables-Llewelyn, owner of R4A for nearly thirty years, had a couple of outings in the car, at Oulton Park and at Donington. He recalls

Sir John Venables-Llewelyn in R12C

R12C as being: "beautifully prepared" and the experience as "great fun and enormously enjoyable". The race at Donington was an unusual one, with two heats of 26 laps on consecutive days, with the driving shared between himself and Tony on both days. He was conscious of some contrasts with his own ERA: "Of course the lack of torque was very noticeable after R4A's beefy two litres! R12C was a good deal heavier and felt it, particularly off the line. Handling with the independent front was not as sharp as R4A; it did not turn in as well and under-steered pretty considerably. However it was not as bad as R4D which used to let its front end hop across the road like a demented kangaroo if you pushed too hard!"

Time for a change: exchanging R12B and R12C

By the mid-1990s, Tony had been racing R12C for more than a decade. Once he had sorted out the handling, so far as he could, and reworked the brakes, it was largely a matter of routine maintenance. He seemed to have reached the limits of any development he could realistically envisage. Bill had also come to a kind of cross roads with R12B: it had been rebuilt and run very successfully during 1994 but he couldn't see any further development of a car he had been racing more or less continuously for three decades. However, he did think some improvements could be made to R12C though it would necessitate a fundamental rebuild.

He therefore suggested to Tony at the VSCC's Donington meeting in August 1994 that R12B and R12C should be swapped in the middle of 1995. R12B was due to go to Australia in the autumn of 1994 and would return from there more or less half way through the 1995 racing season.

Two pictures from Shelsley in July 1994, at a meeting to celebrate the diamond jubilee of both the VSCC and ERA. Rivers Fletcher is opening the hill in R12C. Rivers had seen the original R12B set FTD in September 1936.

Here Tony Stephens is leaving the start, Tony says with rather too much tyre smoke! The Brooklands-type exhaust can just be seen, an accommodation to the concern about noise pollution which introduced a new regime of silencers and noise meters on British hills in the 1990s.

This plan was duly carried through: Tony had his final outing in R12C at the VSCC Mallory Park meeting after which he took the car to Bill, picking up R12B in return.

Full circle: R12C returns to Bill Morris

Bill had a number of objectives for this second major reconstruction. In the first place he wanted to base the car on its 1937 identity when it first appeared as a works C type. He felt that the decision to rebuild the car as Hanuman in the Chula/Bira colours of blue and yellow – which dated back, of course, to the mid-1960s when the whole project was launched – was a mistake. It meant that R12B and R12C were running alongside each other, both in their Bira/Chula colours, which they had never done until 1982. The blue and yellow livery was more appropriate for R12B which had always appeared in that form. Various features of the 1937 car – its paintwork, 18" front wheels and Hartford shock absorbers – would be incorporated in the rebuild.

A second objective was to reduce the weight of the car, as Bill felt it had become too heavy and its performance was suffering as a result. A third aim was to replace any non-original component with proper ERA parts or materials. Among other things, this involved substituting electron-magnesium castings for any aluminium ones the car had previously used. Apart from questions of originality, it would also help with the weight problem. Finally, the handling of the car needed special attention, which would involve looking very closely at the front suspension and steering

R12C: back to 1937

Bill's decision to rebuild the car in its 1937 form meant establishing a new colour scheme. The colour used by the works cars in 1937 is usually described as Dominion Blue. Consulting those who were around at the time (not very numerous, sixty years on) this appeared to be a silvery-blue. Rivers Fletcher, very much one of those who *was* around in 1937, told Bill that the works had stuck some fish scales into blue paint to produce the distinctive colour! Bill thought this had shades of the Heath Robinson about it and "was not the way to go" in the late 1990s. By looking at a number of paint charts he opted for a colour described as Aviation Blue. With the polished silver wheels and exhaust it has undoubtedly produced a distinctive combination, different from any previously used on an ERA. Bill admitted: "It certainly attracted a fair bit of attention: not everyone liked it, but Victoria and I did, so we were happy with it".

Bill with R12C in chassis form in the yard at Leafield during the car's 1995–1998 rebuild. The 18-inch front wheels can be seen.

A further aspect of the car's 1937 identity was its Zoller supercharger. Bill's travails with Zollers have already been outlined along with his decision to opt for a Godfrey unit when reconstructing the car in the 1960s. Bill was not wholly convinced about the Godfrey's merits, quite apart from the fact that its 1937 form seemed to require a Zoller. However he still regarded the latter as a "technical nightmare" and despite spending quite a lot of time and money on various experiments, satisfactory solutions were still elusive. Because of doubts about the Godfrey, and the unresolved issues surrounding the Zoller, Bill's interim solution was to use the standard Jamieson supercharger for R12C's initial re-appearance. Although it was a tight fit it was just possible to squeeze the blower in between the engine and the radiator. Bill's second goal for the rebuild was to reduce the car's weight. He followed the same ground rules as with the Hanuman II rebuild in the mid-1980s: the fuel was held in a bag tank in an aluminium tail, the oil tank was reduced in size and the radiator was lightened. Also contributing to the weight reduction was the substitution of magnesium parts for those that had used other materials in the original 1960s reconstruction: the dashboard and its legs were both replaced in this way. Aluminium rims were used for all four wheels: those at the front were of pre-war manufacture and came from Julian Mazjub, but the rear rims had to be specially built. As Bill didn't weigh the car before or after the rebuild, he doesn't know how much weight was saved.

Making it handle better

Bill knew that R12C's handling had to be improved for the car to be more competitive. His view about the i.f.s. was the same as Tony's: "It's not a very clever design and the combination of a beam axle at the rear and independent suspension at the front makes for rather nasty geometry". He thought that Raymond Mays hadn't appreciated that the Porsche i.f.s system he admired on the Auto Unions was matched with an independent system at the rear via swinging arms. Although Bill thought the C type's i.f.s did cope rather better than the beam axle on rough pre-war tracks its weakness was exposed on the billiard table smooth circuits that prevailed in historic racing. So far as R12C was

Four photos showing the different stages in R12C's 1995–1998 reconstruction.

The first two show the chassis with both axles detached; the engine can be seen on the bench on the right of the picture. The gold star hanging on the wall is one of the plywood stars which were previously on the walls of the White Mouse Garage in Dalling Road, Hammersmith.

The other two photos show a more advanced stage in the rebuild. The axles are now attached to the chassis, part of the steering linkage can be seen and the engine and supercharger are in place but the radiator and bodywork have still to be added; the distinctive new colour scheme is evident in all four pictures.

concerned, Bill acknowledged that Tony had succeeded in sorting out some of the main problems, but his solutions were not always ones Bill was happy with. For example he did not want to continue with the anti-roll bar, as it was not part of any original ERA design. For Bill "rigidity was the name of the game" and this notion guided most of the key alterations. He got Barry Linger to make the thickest torsion bars possible and substituted Hartford dampers which could be locked up solid (they were also much lighter than the hydraulic dampers they replaced). This arrangement produced good results "The torsion bars did just about everything I wanted of them". So much was this the case that it didn't prove necessary in Bill's first two seasons with the car to lock up the Hartfords and his initial settings remained unchanged.

Three important changes were made to the steering. In the first place Bill's study of the pre-war pictures of the C types showed that they

1998: R12C returns to racing.

The first photo was taken at Donington in May 1998, R12C's first appearance following its 1995–1998 rebuild. The i.f.s. no longer incorporates an anti-roll bar and the hydraulic dampers have been replaced by Hartfords.

Bill splashing his way to victory at Oulton Park in June 1998, the car's first win since 1939. He was extremely fast in wet conditions, on this occasion finishing half a minute ahead of runner up Julian Bronson in his Blue Streak Riley, who had sparred with him until a spin ended the duel.

always ran with 18" front wheels. Bill thought his decision to fit 16" rims during the original reconstruction was mistaken. 18" wheels allowed the kingpin point to come out through the centre of the tyres, which could not be achieved with the smaller rims. Secondly the steering was far too high-geared: "every time I corrected a slide I nearly fell off the road in the other direction". The problem in finding someone, *anyone* in fact, with the correct cutting equipment for the all-important worm has been described above. It was Barry Linger who had eventually proved equal to the task, and he now cut a fresh worm which allowed for one and a half turns lock to lock rather than the three-quarters formerly prevailing. Finally Bill played around with adjustments to the steering arms. Tony Stephens had moved the Ackerman point by altering the arms on the front hubs; Bill now had some new arms machined for the idler steering box, very similar to those used on the 308 Alfa, which were both lighter and "looked absolutely fabulous". Unfortunately they proved counter-productive, for Bill had overlooked the fact that the arms are differently attached on the Alfa and the ERA. In the latter's case a ball joint is used and the practical effect was that the new arms twisted and introduced a lot of unwanted play in the steering.

One other matter that received Bill's attention, though it was not on the original agenda, was the gearbox: "I can't leave these damn gearboxes alone". He decided that while the car was in its 'experimental' mode i.e. the first year or two after its reconstruction, he would use a box that was a mixture of road and racing elements. The ratios were those of a close ratio road box, though the big tooth pattern of the racing box was retained. The great attraction of these ratios was that they gave a much lower first gear, which enables good starts as well as reducing strain on the box.

Racing the rebuilt R12C in 1998 and 1999

R12C made its debut in its new form at the Richard Seaman meeting held at Donington in May 1998; inevitably there were a few teething troubles and it didn't come on song properly until a month later at Oulton Park. Here, in very wet conditions, Bill won the 10 lap scratch race which was the first circuit victory for R12C since Bira had won the Nuffield Trophy in 1939. The wet conditions were actually helpful because the remaining handling problems were not so apparent. At the next two meetings they were very obvious: Mallory Park in mid-July was particularly disappointing, with the effort needed to get round some of the corners almost pulling Bill out of his seat. Following the Coys meeting at Silverstone, at the end of July, Bill decided to bring his

R12C in Ireland: an exciting sprint was organised in September 1999 at the Curragh Military Barracks. In addition to the motor racing, there was a gala dinner and the unveiling of a monument commemorating the 50th anniversary of the Curragh International Car Races.

Clockwise from top left: R12C with Bill's sponsor (a monumental mason!) in the driving seat and Bill and Victoria alongside. Bill had been sponsored by many different enterprises over the years, a tombstone maker sponsoring a racing car was a first, he reckoned.

The Curragh Memorial with the Camp Commander. The Memorial had been designed by a daughter of the event's organiser Oliver McCrossan and made by Bill's sponsor.

The Gala Dinner invitation.

Bill inspecting the results which were pinned to a rubbish skip – no unnecessary luxuries! The event was run around and between the army barrack buildings, the sprint course laid out with rope, oil drums and straw bales. Bill was the first competitor on the Sunday morning and rounded the blind final corner, to find the finish line marshal helping an elderly lady across the line; both froze as he swerved around them luckily!

Bourne Celebration, August 1999. To celebrate 100 years since the birth of Raymond Mays, 65 years of ERA and 50 years of BRM a large number of BRMs and ERAs were driven through the streets of Bourne.

Clockwise from top left: In this picture David is in the driving seat while Bill attends to R12C's engine. Note Bill's hat again! Bill did suffer from sunstroke and usually wore a hat. When he and David motored to Spain in 1962 for a short holiday in David's company Jaguar, they had to return to colder Germany due to heat stroke on their first day in the sun!

Bill with Neville Hay at the celebration dinner held to commemorate this triple-anniversary event. They are in front of a picture of Raymond Mays.

David Kergon piloting R12C down one of Bourne's main thoroughfares (by an odd chance Tim May, one of many thousands lining the streets, is at the extreme right of the photo). Bill asked him to demonstrate the car, a pleasant surprise for David who had turned up on his Benelli Sei to spectate, his T-shirt shows an allegiance to Italian bikes. Incidentally, David was to drive R12C for the very first time and was duly cautious, but Bill had forgotten to tell him that the gearbox had an extra low first speed fitted so he nearly hit the aeroscreen, but once on the move it all felt very familiar. The extra low first speed was a 'Bill mod' that was particularly successful. Primarily introduced to reduce wear and maintenance, it usually put him up front into the first corner on circuits and was very helpful for hillclimb starts as well.

107

season to a premature end and put in hand further work on the steering, especially to make it less high-geared.

1999 proved an altogether happier season with the car "nice and reliable", the steering much improved and the results indicating that the car was getting steadily faster. John Ure drove it in the special race at Silverstone to celebrate the 65th anniversary of ERA and finished fourth, with Bill himself taking sixth place in the Hawthorn Spanish Trophy race later in the programme. At the end of the season, Bill won a short scratch race at Cadwell Park – this was actually the last race organised in the twentieth century by the VSCC, and, though he didn't know it at the time, Bill's final race in the U.K.

Just a week after Cadwell a very special event took place in Bourne. A local committee organised a 'heritage day' which in Bourne's case meant a day to celebrate Raymond Mays, ERA and BRM: a hundred years since Mays' birth, sixty five years of ERA and fifty years of BRM. The chief feature of the celebration was the appearance of a large number of ERAs and BRMs which were driven up and down the main streets of Bourne. Bill had committed R12C to be one of the nine ERAs present but the car was actually driven by David Kergon, the first time he had been in its driving seat since collecting the chassis from the docks very nearly thirty-seven years before!

In September R12C crossed the Irish Sea to compete at the Curragh where it won its class. This journey across the water was a foretaste of a much longer one at the beginning of 2000 when it was shipped to Australia. Bill's intention was to undertake a programme of events which would keep the car out of the U.K. until July. Unfortunately, it didn't work out as intended. In an effort to deal with the fact that Australian circuits are a mixture of clockwise and anti-clockwise, Bill had modified R12C's scavenge arrangements which were designed for clockwise circuits. However the modification overloaded the scavenge

Other drivers for R12C:

After Bill's retirement from the driver's seat he continued to enter it for others:

Bill and Victoria push-starting Greg Snape (below right) at Mallala, South Australia.

Greg out on the circuit (below left). Greg drove R12C both in Australia and the UK.

pipes to the tank, burst a hose and all the oil fell out. This caused consternation to those following, but Bill only knew something was wrong when the oil pressure plummeted to zero and the engine went tight. This happened during unofficial practice for the first planned meeting at Philip Island, so it had to be scratched and although R12C went to the Australian Grand Prix, it had to be as a static exhibit.

The car returned to the U.K. in May. Quite apart from the need to repair the Philip Island damage, Bill had further ideas for it, especially the issue of the Zoller supercharger and the possibility of a two litre engine (Raymond Mays had driven R12C with a two litre engine at Phoenix Park in 1937). However, after further thought, Bill decided to retire from the driving seat on his 60th birthday (February 2002) but to retain the car entering it for others to drive. It returned to competition work in 2003/4, initially in Australia with Duncan Ricketts and Greg Snape at the wheel, and then came back to the U.K. for the ERA 70th anniversary race held at Donington in September 2004. Greg Snape, who drove it in that race, undertook some further racing in Australia during 2005 and after the car returned to the U.K. Bill decided to advertise it for sale at the end of 2006 and it was bought by Terry Crabb.

Duncan Ricketts at the wheel at Philip Island in 2004; the spectacular circuit is bounded by the Bass Straits as can be seen in the background.

109

BLUE AND YELLOW

Two seasons racing with B. BIRA

1939 AND 1946

PRINCE CHULA
OF SIAM, G.C.V.O.

One of the books in Bill's collection.
The front cover shows Bira winning the Nuffield Trophy in R12C.

Chapter Five

Reviving and racing Romulus

Romulus – a very special racing car

Although in purely quantative terms, Bill's ERA life was overwhelmingly with R12B and R12C, it was by no means confined to these two cars. In the mid-1970s he had a most interesting period with R2B and in the late 1980s and early 1990s with the E type, GP2. This chapter deals with Bill's involvement with ERA R2B and the following one with GP2.

R2B, the sixth car made by the ERA Company, is far better known by its name – Romulus. It was given this name by its first owner, Prince Birabongse at the beginning of its second year of racing (1936) in order to differentiate it from Remus another very similar ERA (R5B). Although this latter car became famous in its own right, its reputation developed long after it left Prince Bira's stable. Romulus, by contrast, is the car most strongly associated with Prince Bira and his cousin,

A gathering of ERA's at Beaulieu to celebrate the loan of Romulus to the Montagu Memorial Museum in 1965. Identifiable from left to right are: Bertie Brown, Hon. Patrick Lindsay, Peter Brewer, HRH Princess Chula, Dudley Gahagan and Peter Massey, who had just brought R3A from Durban in South Africa. Peter was another Smiths' employee, but was from an earlier graduate intake. R12B was undergoing its major overhaul at this time so was absent on this occasion.

111

HRH. Princess Chula sits in the car, minus her hat, looking relaxed despite the weather.

HRH. Princess Chula looking at Romulus, the car that she and her husband HRH. Prince Chula had been so closely involved with for so long. Note the tail, which is the C Type design entirely for carrying fuel; a modification from the standard B-Type specification.

Prince Chula Chakrabongse, who, with great shrewdness, managed Bira's motor racing.

To put it mildly, the presence of two Asian princes in European motor racing was unusual, unquestionably adding a touch of the exotic to the sport. When it quickly became clear that they were not just rich dilettantes but highly professional and successful, the aura that surrounded them and their activities was further enhanced. The ERA Romulus was the best-known and most successful of their racing cars and consequently always had a particular charisma attached to it.

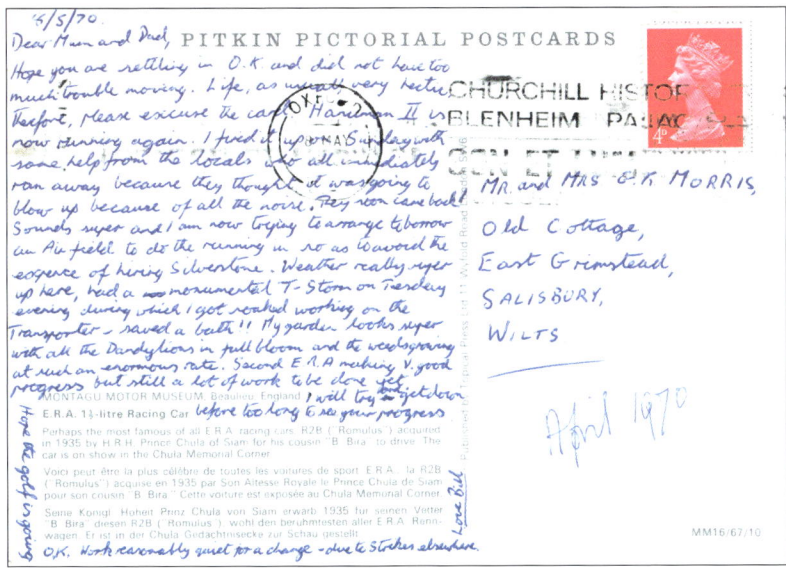

A postcard from Bill: he has filled every conceivable space as he did with all letters and cards. He manages to cram in news about his ERA (reporting that when R12B was fired-up in his yard the locals ran away as they thought it was going to blow-up because of all the noise); about the dandelions growing in his garden; and about a recent thunderstorm "I got soaked working on the transporter – saved a bath!".

Romulus is pictured on the front of the card, displayed at the Montagu Motor Museum against a background of pit equipment, trophies and photos. At a later stage Romulus was assimilated into the general display of racing cars. Bill sent this card to his parents in April 1970 not knowing that just over five years later Romulus would be in his workshop where he would be preparing it to race again.

Restoring Romulus, 1975/6: Photos taken by David Weguelin at Leafield during R2B's rebuild.

Narisa in Romulus (top), pre-restoration.

This shows the car (middle) in its pristine re-spray but with the engine, supercharger and gearbox still to be installed. Narisa (with the appropriate T-shirt!) and Bill alongside.

Bill in R12B Hanuman II (bottom) with Romulus in the background. Bill is wearing his 'best' sweater.

The new silver Hanuman badge (above) has just been fitted to the car.

It had been specially made in Thailand and was an exact replica of the original. Bill looks suitably pleased.

Its special status was intensified because, unlike all their other racing and sports cars, Romulus remained in their ownership up to the 1970s when Bill first became involved. It only made two appearances in the early post-war years and then became a museum piece – literally, firstly in a private museum in Prince Chula's house and then on public show at the Montagu Motor Museum (subsequently National Motor Museum) at Beaulieu.

Bill Morris: the rescue and restoration of Romulus

Romulus had been loaned to the NMM by Princess Chula in 1965; she now owned the car after her husband's death at the end of 1963. Initially Romulus was part of a special exhibition displayed against a background of photos and some of the original pit equipment. At a later stage the car lost this special setting and became one of many others on display. Princess Chula died in 1971 and the car was inherited by Narisa, Prince and Princess Chula's only child.

In addition to dismantling its special exhibition, Narisa found that Romulus was not in good condition, at any rate once the bonnet was lifted – the engine and blower were seized and there was a good deal of corrosion. She knew that her mother had discussed with Bill Romulus' possible restoration and Narisa had got to know Bill herself through David Weguelin, author of the major work on ERA history. Narisa decided that Romulus should be removed from the NMM and transferred to Bill's workshop at Leafield for his restoration. As we noted in the chapter on R12C, Bill was away in South Africa working for Smiths Industries, so it was not until his return that he could begin work.

Describing Bill's role as 'rescuing and restoring' may seem a little over-dramatic but as he himself pointed out, some of the parts were close to disintegration; if they had remained untouched for another year or two, their recovery would have been highly problematic. As it was, although no major component had to be scrapped, one or two elements such as the sump and the sparking plug holes had suffered water damage and had to be carefully repaired. The car was stripped to its bare chassis and what followed was summarised by Roger Richmond, who was closely involved with the whole operation: "The rebuild was mainly a question of attention to bearings, of cleaning and general refettling, and two large rotary wire brushes were worn out in the process of removing thirty years disuse. No major parts were replaced, although the gearbox internals were of the early type, and were replaced with the normal gearing used on the B types" ('Romulus Returns', *VSCC Bulletin*, Spring 1977).

116

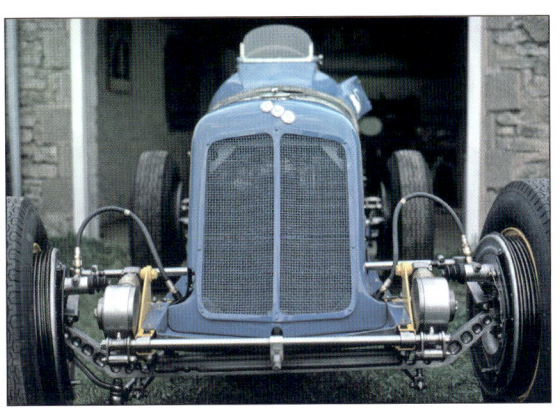

These pictures shows different stages in Romulus' restoration.

The top two (facing page) illustrate the rather distressed state of its engine and blower mounting when it arrived at Leafield. The middle three display its pristine chassis following cleaning and respraying together with the re-assembly of the front axle. The bottom two show further stages in the rebuilding with the tail now in place followed by a picture of the distinctive blue-faced instruments which have been refitted to the dashboard.

The five pictures on this page show further important stages on the road to completion. In the top left hand picture can be seen the various badges celebrating Romulus' racing successes in the 1930s; then follow three pictures which show most of the main body panels have been fitted and the bottom end of the engine installed. The middle picture on the right demonstrates Romulus' De Ram dampers and its hydraulic brakes. The bottom picture could be titled 'Mission Completed!' as the fully restored car is on its trailer ready to depart for its Silverstone 'debut'.

Romulus (R2B) back out with Hanuman (R12B) and Remus (R5B) in line at Silverstone at the May meeting, 1976.

118

Silverstone practice. In the early days of learning about ERAs, brake grab was a common difficulty, until Bill decided to file off a substantial part of their linings' leading edge. This cured the problem and here is Bill applying his remedy to Romulus.

Romulus races for the first time since 1948

Romulus' first event was the VSCC's traditional 'opener' at Silverstone. Unlike the low–profile re-emergence of the E type (described in the next chapter) a similar quiet beginning for Romulus was hardly likely, given its 'celebrity' status and that it hadn't turned a racing wheel since 1948.

In fact it was decided to capitalise on the car's return to racing by organising a small exhibition in the paddock displaying trophies Romulus had won, together with various other memorabilia. The car and the exhibition aroused wide interest as shown by the £300 raised for a cancer charity through the sale of raffle tickets and associated donations. Romulus' re-appearance was duly noted by the press with front-cover or large portrait pictures of Bill and the car 'at work'.

The Bira/Chula Exhibition at Silverstone, May 1976. To mark Romulus' re-appearance many of Bira and Chula's trophies together with photographs and other memorabilia were exhibited in a small tent. Raffle tickets were sold and £300 raised for a cancer charity.

119

On the front cover Romulus' return to racing attracted much interest. Terence Brettell's close-up of Bill 'at work' was used for the front cover of the summer 1976 VSCC Bulletin.

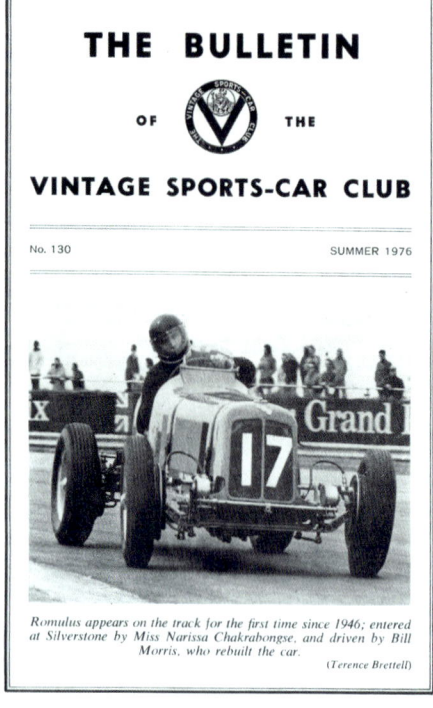

Motor Sport similarly headed its report with a large colour shot of Bill and R2B. The London Evening News gave prominence to Romulus' re-appearance at Silverstone as can be seen in its issue of 29 April 1976.

The competitive part of the meeting was also successful: a subsequent programme note said Romulus "surprised everyone by its speed". For much of the All Comers race it was among the leading six cars and although it fell back towards the end with magneto problems, by any reckoning this was a most encouraging beginning, or beginning again.

The remainder of 1976: from strength to strength

Romulus' next event, the VSCC Oulton Park meeting, demonstrated that its speed at Silverstone was no flash in the pan. Indeed it was a double demonstration of Romulus' speed *and* reliability as Bill piloted him to third in the Seaman Historic race and fourth in the All Comer's race. In the Seaman race Bill was second on the grid and led off as the flag dropped remaining in the lead for "three inspiring tyre-burning laps". Bill was then overtaken by Martin Morris, the eventual winner, but held on to second place until half-distance when Patrick Lindsay went by. In the All Comers race – a twenty lap race round the shortened Oulton track (1.65 miles) – he was the first pre-war car to finish. Bill had expressed some slight anxiety about the brakes prior to the Oulton

Romulus and Remus battling it out! Although Romulus bears the same number (9) two different races are involved. This picture is the 1976 Seaman Historic Race at Oulton Park and Patrick Lindsay is just overtaking Bill; they finished second and third.

This photo was taken a month or so later at the VSCC's second Silverstone meeting. Here the positions are reversed with Bill leading Patrick. Romulus' rear wheel is working very hard but to good effect as Bill won this pre-War All-Comers scratch race and Patrick had to settle for second place.

races, emphasising that there hadn't been sufficient racing miles for them to be properly bedded-in. At the earlier Silverstone meeting the *VSCC Bulletin*'s reporter had found him filing away at the linings to try and eliminate brake-grab, Bill declaring if that didn't work "he would oil them". By the time the two Oulton races were completed brake problems were well on the way to being solved.

At the second VSCC Silverstone Romulus excelled himself – helped by his driver, of course! – and won the Pre-War All Comers race; Bill took the lead on the first lap at Becketts and wasn't subsequently challenged. Just as at Oulton there was a second bite at the cherry with an entry in the Hawthorn Memorial Trophy race. Romulus' owner, Narisa, was watching this race and thought that her father, Prince Chula, might have protested at the starting position of Pat Lindsay and *Remus* as the car's wheels were rather ahead of the line. However, any notion she might do the same was quickly squashed when she saw "her driver's start in Romulus which was "competitive" to put it mildly and took him straight past all the cars on the second row of the grid" (*VSCC Bulletin* 131, Winter 1976). Bill finished sixth overall and, as at Oulton, he was the first pre-war car.

During the Hawthorn race, Bill's initial fifth station had given way to Frank Lockhart's assault in the unique Rover Special and they disputed the places again at Cadwell at the end of August. At this stage of what turned out to be a very long competitive life, Frank and the Rover were a quick combination, provoking Bill Boddy to wonder whether "we shall all soon be wanting to drive Rovers". Bill and Romulus led the whole pack from the start but Simon Phillips in a Cooper-Bristol went by on the second lap and the main interest was the scrap for second and third spots between Bill and Frank. There was constant passing and re-passing but Bill managed to hold on to the runner's up position at the flag, the crowd applauding both drivers for such an exciting race.

Narisa provided a much-appreciated bottle of champagne at the conclusion of the Cadwell meeting to celebrate Bill finishing as runner-up in the *Motor Sport* Brooklands Memorial Trophy (an annual competition). Further alcoholic imbibing was a prominent feature of a trip to Ireland, for a meeting at Phoenix Park, which was Romulus' final event in its 1976 programme. Even the car joined in as Roger Richmond reported that with a high axle ratio Romulus was pulling 6000 RPM on the long straight, equivalent to 135 mph, and "drinking methanol at nearly a gallon a minute!" (*VSCC Bulletin*, no. 133, Spring 1977). The human drinking was not timed but probably a little slower though there was no doubt "that a good time was had by all". The car turned in two good results again finishing second in the Pre-War race and 6th when it mixed it with the post-war brigade.

first lap which dropped him well down. Unfortunately just after half-distance Romulus' magneto gave up and Bill first dropped back and then retired. While it lasted, Bill found it an exciting and highly distinctive experience: he took much tighter lines in order to manoeuvre if the need arose and was very conscious of the historical weight on his shoulders driving the car in which Bira had scored his first major victory and on the circuit where it had been secured.

Another significant aspect of the Monaco expedition was that it marked the debut, if we can put it in that way, of John Ure, who had hitched his way down and attached himself to the

Bill's pass for the Monaco event.

It was on this circuit that Bira had his first major victory with Romulus.

White Mouse équipe. Roger Richmond, an established member of the team, concluded his account of Monaco by reporting that when they were relaxing at a kerbside café enjoying the parade of beautiful ladies and beautiful cars "one member of the party suggested that if we had some decent beer as well it might almost be better than sitting outside the "Green Man" after a vintage Silverstone meeting" (*VSCC Bulletin*, no 143, Autumn 1979). No higher praise could be imagined!

1980 and beyond: occasional appearances and a return to the museum

Bill only drove Romulus on four other occasions before the car returned to a museum, though it was to Narisa's London Toy and Model Museum, not the NMM.

There were two outings in 1980, and one each in 1981 and 1984. Romulus' first appearance in 1980 was at Oulton Park for the Seaman Historic race which was run in wet conditions. The race was fairly processional with the three leading cars taking up station early on; Bill finished third behind the two-litre ERAs of Patrick Lindsay and Martin Morris. Romulus' second race in 1980 was at Silverstone where there was more dispute: Day led off in the two-litre R14B, but Bill overtook on the second lap and was able to keep ahead of Donald, convincing Roger Richmond, who was again chronicling the meeting for the *VSCC Bulletin*, "that a thoroughly original ERA is the best formula for winning races, Bill Morris emphasising the point by putting up the fastest lap". Rather interestingly he judged that Bill was better round the corners than R14B, despite Romulus having no limited slip differential. Bill's final win with Romulus came in April 1981 when Bill was beaten off the line by the Bentley-Napier, but soon put that to rights. By the third lap he had a big lead and was going sufficiently quickly to have lapped half the field before the race ended.

The next time Romulus appeared was at the special race to celebrate ERA's golden anniversary in July 1984. The car had not been used in the intervening three years but Bill was still able to put in a good performance finishing seventh overall with Brian Classic, Willie Green and Patrick Marsh ahead of him in $1\frac{1}{2}$ litre cars; the first three cars were all two litre-powered. The car was entered, with Bill as driver, for the similar race run in 1994 but it non-started.

A few years before the 1994 ERA race, Bill had been involved with Romulus again in the autumn of 1987 when Narisa withdrew him from the museum to prepare for the expedition to Thailand. The plan was for Narisa to drive Romulus at Donington as a form of 'training' for doing the same in Thailand at the Bangkok Grand Prix. Everything went to plan, more or less, and Narisa drove the car at Donington, albeit in poor weather, which she certainly didn't expect to encounter in Thailand. Romulus was duly transported to Thailand and became the central figure in the expedition described in Chapter Three and memorably captured in the film '*Romulus returns to Siam*'.

After the Thailand trip Romulus returned to the U.K. and was looked after privately, though he was on public display at the two subsequent ERA anniversary races in 1999 and 2004. In 2007 he was sold to Gregory Whitten and now resides in the U.S.A.

Quite apart from his racing exploits with Bill at the wheel, Romulus' re-appearance occupied quite a lot of space in the enthusiast's 'bible', *Motor Sport*. It's worth recalling what this was all about as Bill was a lively contributor to the discussion and the issues raised are in no way peculiar to Romulus, but have a much wider resonance within the whole world of historic motor sport.

Should Romulus have been revived?

For many people Romulus' revival was entirely pleasurable: certainly this was true for his owner (Narisa), his driver (Bill) and all the 'crew' (prominent among who were Bill's brother, Ben Morris, Roger Richmond and Tony Stephens). Although a lot of hard work was involved to get the car going again, once that was done, Romulus maintained his pre-war reputation of being a fast and reliable racing car. Fellow competitors had another significant rival on the grid and spectators were able to enjoy the sight and sound of a car that most had never seen and, prior to 1976, thought they were unlikely ever to see on a racing track.

However, not everyone was pleased. A correspondent in *Motor Sport* set the ball rolling for what Roger Richmond called "the museum party". He wanted Romulus: "to rest on its many laurels... and not be dragged out again for a 'club' meeting... If Miss Chakrabongse is so keen for it to be raced perhaps she could persuade Bira to drive it...". This set two hares running – not just whether Romulus should be racing but whether Bira, rather than Bill, should be driving him. Denis Jenkinson signed himself up to run after both hares: "I do agree that Bira's famous ERA Romulus should not have been dragged into 'club' racing... By all means clean it up and get it running, rather than let it moulder in the precincts of the NMM but... how much more it would have meant if B. Bira had given us some demonstration laps for old times' sake. To be hacked around the Silverstone Club Circuit in company with a lot of well-meaning amateurs must have seemed rather undignified for a car that had previously only ever raced in serious competition".

Oulton Park 1980

Bill's response to these comments began with a no-nonsense statement about the seriousness of Romulus' condition: "had Romulus continued to remain as he was, he would have been very perforated and in a very sorry state within the next five years….Romulus' sump, blower drive housing, gearbox casing, differential housing, bell housing and supercharger parts are of electron manufacture and all these parts were in a serious state due to internal corrosion, so much so that both the sump and the blower drive housing were within an ace of being eaten through". Bill went on to point out that the way to prevent those parts from similar deterioration in the future was to flush them regularly with fresh oil and "the best way of doing that is to run him occasionally".

On the Bira argument, Bill said "Prince Bira is fully aware of Romulus' return to the circuits as are all the original "White Mouse" stable personnel. They are all as enthusiastic as ever and I believe they are very proud still to be associated and even more proud of Narisa Chakrabongse following in her father's footsteps and taking active steps to maintain this island's racing heritage"

There was every sign that what Roger Richmond described as "a nice meaty argument" could run on... and on, providing enough material to fill numerous column inches of *Motor Sport* (Bill Boddy indicated that many letters had flowed in on the subject). One of the letters Bill did print was from Lord Montagu who sought to justify his museum's practice of benign neglect on the grounds that Princess Chula wanted the car to "remain in exactly the same state as when she and her late husband inhibited it and put it to rest" and that she was "adamantly against racing". Those may indeed have been Princess Chula's sentiments in 1965 when Romulus first went to Beaulieu but by the early 1970s she had changed her mind. In July 1971 she wrote to David and Bill agreeing to their removing the car from the museum to strip it down and assess "the costs of rebuilding to Hanuman II standards". It is therefore very likely that but for Princess Chula's death Romulus' restoration would have been brought forward by three or four years.

Bill Boddy was himself not convinced by the arguments of the "museum party" but he gave Jenks further space later in the year to set out his stall in more detail. By this stage the 'Bira as driver' line had faded away but Jenks still didn't want Romulus either raced or driven by anyone else: "It was a very special ERA and it was unique. It is still a very special ERA but some of its character has gone. It is no longer the ERA *as* Bira last drove it, it is now an immaculately rebuilt ERA, immaculately driven by Bill Morris and still very successful."

There was a fascinating footnote to this debate a few years later. Jenks was in action again on ERA with an article to celebrate the golden anniversary year. Towards the end he tells us, "You don't find ERAs in museums, you must go to a racing circuit to see them… Racing cars in museums are all very well, but there is nothing like seeing and hearing them in full flight… " (*Motor Sport*, September 1984). Not surprisingly Bill couldn't resist such an open target and he took aim: "Finally isn't it interesting how even 'dyed-in-the-wool' experts such as D.S.J. change their views after a few years. At the finish of his article he extols the fact that all the ERAs are out and about and you don't find ERAs in museums… . Yet eight years ago he was castigating Prince Chula's daughter Narisa for allowing me to give R2B Romulus a bit of an overhaul and a repaint and for letting me drive it. Well Romulus is back in a museum now. Damn it, Jenks won again" (*Motor Sport*, November 1984). If not a bull's eye, pretty close!

Chapter Six

Racing an E type, 1989-1993

The E type ERA – high hopes not fulfilled

The E type ERA has not had a good press. Doug Nye included it among what he called his *Motor Racing Mavericks* and Norman Smith's *Case History,* after describing Peter Walker's crash in the Isle of Man, concludes "Thus it can truthfully be said that the E type ERA, once heralded with a blaze of hope, ended in a blaze – not one of victory or glory – but a blaze just the same!". Norman Smith wrote that in the late 1950s and although he acknowledged that some 'resurrection' had taken place with the hybrid ERA-Jaguar he wasn't very optimistic about its prospects.

The ERA-Jaguar was the first visible sign that anything had survived of the two E types that raced in the first few years after the Second World War. Their origins lay in the 1938-9 period, though only one car (GP1) was completed, which competed at Albi in July 1939 where it demonstrated great speed but failed to finish. Although all the parts existed in 1939 for the second E type, GP2, it wasn't built up until 1946.

Humphrey Cook re-constituted the ERA Company in 1946 but as he did not intend to have a works team, both E types were sold to private owners. Although they managed to finish some races they were prone to mechanical failure and neither came any where near rivalling either the speed or, particularly, the reliability of the earlier ERAs.

For the first half of the 1950s, both E types more or less disappeared. It was Ken Flint and Verdun Edwards, garage-owners based in Liverpool, who re-introduced them to competition work using GP1's chassis and GP2's body – suitably adapted – with a Jaguar XK120 engine to create the ERA-Jaguar sports car in 1955. After a few teething troubles, this combination achieved modest success in club-type events. Subsequently Flint and Edwards developed other interests and the E types were advertised in February 1958.

Enter Gordon Chapman

GP1 was sold to Jim Berry, a noted amateur racer with Bugattis and an ERA Special, and GP2 to John Nicholson. It was at about this time that

The owner and his 'jockey':

Gordon Chapman and Bill had known each other for many years before their joint endeavours with the E-type.

This photo was taken some years before that collaboration began.

Gordon Chapman became interested in the E type and in 1959 he bought GP1's chassis from Jim Berry. Gordon had owned R2A, ERA's second chassis, since 1957 and had had some good results with it. But he wasn't resting on his laurels and he had an ambitious scheme to re-create the two E types in their original form – as single-seater ERA racing cars. This goal took a very long time to realise and couldn't really start properly until he acquired GP2. This chassis had evolved in a similar way to GP1 as John Nicholson created a sports car from it powered by a Jaguar engine and clothed in an all-enveloping Williams and Pritchard body.

As we have already noted in the chapter dealing with R12C's recreation, it was this car that both Gordon and Bill encountered in the mid-1960s: Bill was acquiring an ERA rev counter and Gordon all the rest! Bill did not recognise GP2's chassis underneath its streamlined body shell, but even if he had, he probably would not have been tempted, whereas for Gordon it was a crucial step forward in his plan to re-create both E types.

Gordon laboured away during the 1970s and by the early 1980s both cars were sufficiently advanced to commission new bodies which were crafted by Duncan Ricketts. In July 1984 there was a special race organised by the VSCC to commemorate the 50th anniversary of ERA and Gordon brought both E types to Silverstone for their first public showing since he began the restoration. GP2 was considerably more advanced than GP1 and was entered for the race whereas GP1 was displayed on its trailer minus most of its 'internals'. In fact GP2 wasn't really quite at the point where it was ready for active competition and after the warming-up lap it was withdrawn from the race itself.

Bill Morris drives GP2

Another four years went by which included a period when Gordon lent GP2 to Tom Wheatcroft's Grand Prix Car Collection at Donington. At the beginning of 1989 Bill was without an ERA to drive, as R12B had been damaged in the accident in New Zealand. Gordon Chapman who had known Bill for many years asked him whether he would help to get the car race-worthy, an important part of which would involve driving it in various events. Bill was happy to do this and things were sufficiently advanced for Gordon to put in an entry for the Richard Seaman Historic Trophy Race in July 1989.

As previous chapters have noted, this race was the VSCC's premier trophy event for historic racing cars and had been based at Oulton Park since 1956. When Bill first became involved the head was off the engine and after Bill had helped Gordon to put it back tuning began to achieve racing performance. This was far from straightforward; Bill's own account written shortly after the Oulton Park meeting describes the problems:

"Gordon Chapman and I had much trouble leading up to Oulton Park trying to determine (1) How much oil to feed to the Zoller supercharger so that it would not seize (2) What needles to use in the S.U.

Bill at Oulton Park, 1 June 1989. This was GP2's first appearance in Bill's hands. John Ure and Gordon Chapman are among the pushers.

Bill is in the paddock at Oulton (still with some grass in those days). Both in practice and in the race itself there were various engine problems which kept Gordon and Bill busy.

carbs and (3) What heat range of Lodge plugs to use. Up to the time we arrived at Oulton Park, although we had it running cleanly it would not stay clean and invariably either oiled or wet its plugs over about 4000 rpm".

It was hoped that in the practice period at Oulton they could make some solid progress but GP2 remained intransigent until the third of Bill's qualifying laps when "it suddenly chimed in on six cylinders half way round a corner and spat me up the road in a big spin from whence I watched the rest of practice". Bill was able to do another lap, but it was untimed and the engine was still not running cleanly.

With the prospect of the race itself looming only an hour or two later, it was now unavoidably time for decisions: "So in went much leaner needles and much softer plugs, the car ran on six cylinders in the paddock and warmed up nicely, so with much trepidation we lined up at the back of the grid. The warm up lap went O.K., still on six and at the flag drop I made up about three rows of the grid before I could go no further and then it bloody rained. At this point I found we had virtually NO grip anywhere, chronic wheelspin away from the corners, little braking, and even less grip in the corners, so the rest of the race was spent trying to keep a now six-cylinder E type out of the bushes. At about half distance, we were still on six and I was beginning to get the hang of things a little; then it started baulking on second to third upward changes, so I then stayed in third and top and started going famously and finished on six cylinders".

When Bill had finished the race, Gordon told him the tyres were ten years old which doubtless had been a major factor in some of the problems he describes. He certainly found that GP2 was a distinctive experience quite different from its ERA predecessors, indeed not like a pre-war car at all but "very similar to a P25 BRM". He liked the gearbox – "super synchro gearbox with a very close ratio between second and third" but not the task of "turning little taps on and off to keep the blower lubricated on the fast straights".

Bill finished 10th with a best lap of 2:25:3; the leading drivers were lapping considerably faster (under two minutes), but they were all driving established race-proven cars. Bill was handling a car that had last raced in 1950 and which had undergone virtually no testing in its rebuilt form – Bill was now doing the testing in actual races!

Progress with GP2

As he said following Oulton, "it will improve" and it clearly did. Gordon entered it for Cadwell Park and Donington, the two remaining VSCC circuit meetings in 1989. By Cadwell matters had improved considerably as Bill finished third in the Pre-War All Comers Race. The sight and sound of GP2 greatly appealed to Terence Brettell who reported the meeting for the *VSCC Bulletin*. He noted that to begin with the E type was well up with the leaders but it lost contact somewhat as the race progressed though in no way diminishing Terence's enthusiasm: "what a beautiful car the E type is and how good to see it going well".

GP2's debut at Oulton was certainly not accompanied by any great blaze of publicity, the programme preview didn't mention it as a novel entry and similarly the VSCC *Bulletin* said nothing about its appearance

Cadwell Park, August 1989: this was Bill's second drive with GP2 and its flowing lines are shown to good effect. Bill finished third in the pre-War All Comers' race.

in the Seaman race. However by Cadwell the car – and its owner and driver – were getting rather more attention and Terence Brettell's report was accompanied by two pictures.

Perhaps the car needed to hide its light under a bushel, at any rate at Donington it suffered an attack of what might be called the 'The Curse of the E type' or 'E Type hoodoo'. Bill's pit wondered why he appeared to be waving to them on the starting grid; after the rest of the field had departed they discovered he was displaying the gear lever which had broken off in his hand when he engaged first gear!

The breakage was blamed on faulty workmanship when the part had originally been made. Gordon Chapman crafted a replacement but this broke as well – possibly because Gordon had too enthusiastically embraced the idea of 'lightening' it. This incident happened in practice at the second VSCC Silverstone meeting in June 1990, which was the car's first event that year. Fortunately it didn't prevent Bill running in the Hawthorn Spanish Trophy race in which he finished 6th, a more than respectable result and another indication that GP2 was able to finish the races in which it started, summed up by a picture caption saying: "Bill Morris makes ERA history in an E type by finishing another race".

Steady progress continued at GP2's two other meetings in 1990, Oulton Park and Cadwell. In the Seaman Historic Trophy race he finished 8th and the gap between the leading cars and GP2 was much narrower than the previous year. At Cadwell, GP2 ran in two races finishing fifth and second – admittedly the field in the latter race was small but it meant that GP2 had run more than satisfactorily in two ten lap races within the same event and Gordon Chapman's pleasure was evident.

Bill in the Seaman Historic Trophy in 1990. He is coming up Clay Hill at Oulton Park pursued by Chris Mayman in AJM1 who eventually overtook Bill to finish seventh with Bill eighth in GP2.

Cadwell Park in August 1990.

GP2 emerging from the scrutineering bay with Bill's helmet receiving the once-over from Scrutineer Geoff Sheppard.

Gordon and Bill are busy cleaning the bodywork after GP2 had generated a certain amount of oil surge. It was a successful day for GP2, Bill and Gordon with a second and a fifth.

Later years with GP2

GP2 did not appear again until August 1992. Gordon was working on the car and when it competed in the Seaman race, held rather later than usual at the end of August, its engine was listed as 1496cc rather than the 1976cc it had been in 1989/90. The car in fact had exactly the same engine but Bill had checked its dimensions and discovered it was half a litre less than Gordon had initially reckoned (Gordon had many gifts but the higher mathematics was not among them). Both Gordon and Bill enjoyed this revelation! It's worth noting, too, that the car was still using its Zoller supercharger which Bill had found somewhat distracting on the initial drive at Oulton – "turning little taps on and off to keep the blower lubricated on fast straights". The chapter on R12C has outlined all the problems Bill faced in trying to devise a Zoller set-up for that car during its re-build and his eventual abandonment of the idea in favour of a Godfrey installation. On GP2 the arrangement seemed to work and did not cause either of the retirements Bill experienced. It wasn't perfect, however and as noted below it was one aspect of GP2 that he would have tried to improve if he'd had a free hand with the car.

When Bill took to the wheel again in 1992-3 GP2 performed pretty much as it had done two years before. For example Bill finished 6th in the Hawthorn Spanish Trophy race in 1993, the same position as in 1990. The gap between his best lap and that of the winner was six seconds in the earlier race, four in the latter; the narrowing almost certainly reflecting a slightly slower winning speed in 1993 than in 1990. At the Oulton meeting in 1992, like the Cadwell event in 1990, GP2 ran in two races finishing 6th in one and 4th in the other. His fourth came in a 12 lap All Comers' race where he was 7th at the end of the first lap and fifth at half distance – through overtaking two other cars. Finally he moved up to fourth when the leading car dropped out.

One interesting feature of the 1993 programme was an entry for the VSCC Prescott meeting. No E type had competed at Prescott before and indeed none has since. Whether the idea was Bill's or Gordon's doesn't seem quite clear at this distance, but as we have seen Prescott was always the exception to Bill's lack of interest in hill climbs and sprints. Bill finished second in the 1101–1500cc class with a best run of 44.45, a very good time for a car that was wholly untested on hill climbs and whose gearbox was not working entirely satisfactorily – there were problems in selecting first gear.

Over the four seasons Bill drove GP2 there were only two mechanical retirements – the broken gear lever already mentioned in 1990 and the 1993 Seaman Historic race when he just failed to make the distance by dropping out on the penultimate lap. So GP2 was able to overcome some of the conventional wisdom about the E type – that if it was entered in a race it was quite likely it wouldn't start and if it *did* start even more likely that it wouldn't finish. Its results were respectable rather than outstanding because it was never fully competitive with the fastest ERAs of the late 1980s/early 1990s. For it to have had any chance of contesting the odds with such cars it would have needed much more development – Bill mentions particularly the need for some general lightening, various aspects of the blower which required attention and improvements to the brakes to make them as good as those on Hanuman II.

Three photos taken at Prescott in August 1993.

The first shows Bill preparing to come out of the paddock to the start line, with Gordon, Lucy and Narisa Chapman looking on.

The second is taken just after the start with the Orchard car park, the Bugatti Trust building and the Gloucestershire countryside in the background.

The third picture is of Bill exiting Orchard Corner. Bill's best run – 4.45 – was second fastest in the 1101–1500cc Class. This was the only time an E-type has competed at Prescott.

Two Silverstone events for GP2

The top picture is of GP2 in 1999 when Bill drove it in the ERA 65th Anniversary Race. Bill is just putting his glasses on, prior to settling himself in the car; to the left is R12C with John Ure at the wheel.

This was taken the previous year, 1998, when there was a commemoration of the 1948 British Grand Prix. GP2 is alongside Duncan Ricketts' GP1; Gordon Chapman's daughters, Lucy and Narisa are between the two E-types. ERA R1A and a 6C Maserati can be glimpsed further back.

An important difference between GP1 and GP2 is in the transmission: in GP1 the driver sits lower and further back than in GP2. This difference reflects the stepped-down transmission in GP1, a feature of its design making it more complicated and potentially troublesome.

Afterwards…

As described in the Hanuman II chapters, R12B returned to the fray in 1994 and Bill's energies were fully deployed as entrant and preparer, to be succeeded in turn, in 1995, by the major rebuild of R12C. Unfortunately, Gordon Chapman's health began to deteriorate so the development of GP2 came to an end. The car appeared at the 60th celebration of ERA in 1994 but as a 'non-combatant' that is it was on display but didn't take part in the special race for ERA cars. Five years later, in 1999, there was a similar race and this time it did run and Bill was at the wheel. It had had little or no 'exercise' in the intervening years so it wasn't in any state to be driven competitively.

After Chapman's death, GP2 passed to his daughters, Lucy and Narisa, and it has been on loan to the Donington Museum for most of the time, though in the summer of 2008 it was 'liberated' and fired-up (after quite a lot of fettling) for some demonstration laps at Silverstone and the following year it was similarly demonstrated at the Goodwood Revival. The necessary fettling was the work of Duncan Ricketts and his nephew James who by this time knew a considerable amount about E types, as Duncan had bought GP1, following Gordon's death, from his widow. Jeannie Chapman had asked Bill as one of Gordon's closest friends to help in disposing of her late husband's cars. Bill therefore played a part in the sale of GP1; subsequently Bill himself bought and took on another of Gordon's very interesting projects, which was to complete and race the 1954 Kieft V8 Grand Prix car that the original company had never brought to fruition. Duncan Ricketts completed the restoration of the first E type, GP1, begun by Gordon, and has now been racing the car for more than ten years. He has more engineering and racing experience of the E type than anyone else and maybe, at some future stage, some of this will contribute to the racing development of GP2, with which Gordon and Bill took the first important steps between 1989-1993.

Chapter Seven

ERA man in and out of the workshop

So far, in chronicling Bill's life with ERAs, we have concentrated on his involvement with the four cars that he worked on and drove competitively – R12B, R12C, R2B and GP2. In this chapter we are casting the net a little wider in order to capture some other aspects of Bill's life connected to ERA and the wider field of historic racing.

Pre-selectors and all that

One inescapable fact of life for the great majority is the need to earn a living – only a tiny minority have sufficient wealth to absolve them from this necessity and Bill certainly wasn't among them. He was still an apprentice at Smiths Industries when he became an ERA owner and he knew that he had to earn his own bread and butter and generate enough to fund his motor racing. Once he graduated from Smiths Industries' training programme he worked for them in a variety of jobs until the late 1970s. One of these jobs involved managing a plant at Witney in Oxfordshire and it was this posting that led him to buy a cottage at Leafield, a small village a few miles from Witney. Once established here, the racing cars, their spares and all the equipment were moved from their previous base in Lancaster Mews in London.

The Leafield house known simply for many years as 'Lower End', was quite a small cottage, but had the great bonus of various outbuildings as well as a reasonable plot of land attached to it. To begin with, these outbuildings housed Hanuman II, the chassis of R12C and all the various spares and workshop equipment. At a later stage Bill was able to extend these outbuildings, relatively unobtrusively, to give him more workshop space which was particularly necessary once he left Smiths Industries and launched into self-employment.

Initially he took on work for a local wildlife park maintaining their collection of Land Rovers. Subsequently, he became the successor to Cyril Turnell, who for many years had been 'the gearbox man' for most ERA owners. Turnell's role in keeping ERA gearboxes in good order has already been alluded to in Chapter Three. ERA used the pre-selector designed by Major W.G. Wilson, which was manufactured by companies closely associated with Armstrong Siddeley. Cyril Turnell originally worked for one of these companies – Self Changing Gears – but after he retired he mostly operated from what Bill described as 'his garden shed'.

Bill took over his business in 1987 and became a major source for the overhaul of pre-selectors and the provision of all relevant spare parts. Although he bought up pre-selector gearbox parts whenever he found them, there weren't that many around by the mid -1980s so Bill had to commission new parts through specialist manufacturers. Quite apart from ERAs, a number of other racing and road cars – including post-war, Connaught and HWM – fitted pre-selectors and many of these boxes passed through Bill's workshop. By the time Bill sold his business, he had overhauled around three hundred and fifty pre-selector gearboxes. He kept a slightly battered W.H. Smith cash book in which he listed in some detail every single box he dealt with – whether they were ENV (most usually the 75 or 110) or Armstrong Siddeley, what parts needed replacing and the customer's name. Almost every make of car that used a pre-selector pre or post war can be found in these pages – in addition to those just mentioned there are examples of Alta, Invicta, Lagonda, MG, Riley, Squire and Talbot in addition to a few Bentleys or Maseratis which, atypically, had been fitted with a pre-selector.

Bill didn't by any means confine his efforts to a 'simple' overhaul, if indeed there was such a process. As the preceding discussions of R12B and R12C have made clear he was always anxious to experiment –

Bill at work on one of the numerous gearboxes that received his attention during the 1980s and 1990s.

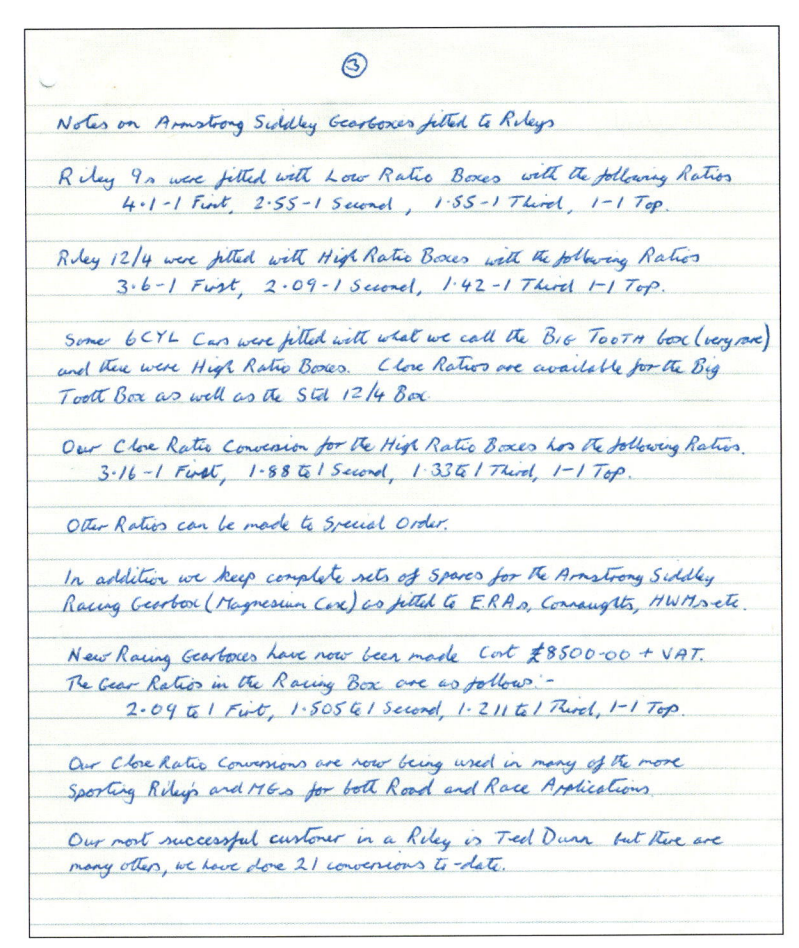

> ③
>
> Notes on Armstrong Siddley Gearboxes fitted to Rileys
>
> Riley 9s were fitted with Low Ratio Boxes with the following Ratios
>   4.1-1 First, 2.55-1 Second, 1.55-1 Third, 1-1 Top.
>
> Riley 12/4 were fitted with High Ratio Boxes with the following Ratios
>   3.6-1 First, 2.09-1 Second, 1.42-1 Third, 1-1 Top.
>
> Some 6 CYL Cars were fitted with what we call the BIG TOOTH box (very rare) and these were High Ratio Boxes. Close Ratios are available for the Big Tooth Box as well as the Std 12/4 Box.
>
> Our Close Ratio Conversion for the High Ratio Boxes has the following Ratios.
>   3.16-1 First, 1.88 to 1 Second, 1.33 to 1 Third, 1-1 Top.
>
> Other Ratios can be made to Special Order.
>
> In addition we keep complete sets of Spares for the Armstrong Siddley Racing Gearbox (Magnesium Case) as fitted to ERAs, Connaughts, HWMs etc.
>
> New Racing Gearboxes have now been made Cost £8500-00 + VAT. The Gear Ratios in the Racing Box are as follows:-
>   2.09 to 1 First, 1.505 to 1 Second, 1.211 to 1 Third, 1-1 Top.
>
> Our Close Ratio Conversions are now being used in many of the more Sporting Rileys and MGs for both Road and Race Applications.
>
> Our most successful customer in a Riley is Ted Dunn but there are many others, we have done 21 conversions to-date.

A page from Bill's notebook summarising details of various Riley pre-selector gearboxes and the availability of spares for boxes fitted to ERA, Connaught and HWM.

"I can't leave these damn gearboxes alone" – and increasing numbers of his customers were requesting modifications to their boxes similar to those Bill made to R12C's in 1995-8. Such procedures only increased the complexity of the whole business and in the 'workbook' listing all the gearboxes he dealt with there is a list of gearbox parts that amounts to some 140 items.

While gearboxes undoubtedly absorbed a lot of Bill's time and energy, they didn't exhaust it. Someone who knew him well over most of his adult life said: "The theme all the way was energy plus strong commercial instincts". He was alert to a business opportunity whenever it presented itself as for example when he took on the sole British agency for Vertex magnetos, after having experienced supply problems with magnetos for his ERAs.

His commercial instinct also ensured that he kept a close eye on his business accounts; like most self-employed people Bill used accountants but he always had a pretty good idea about his trading position.

Towcars and Transporters: the Ford F100 has been pictured earlier – here are a variety of other variations on that theme:

Roger Richmond's Rolls-Royce with Tony Stephens at the wheel and attached to no less than three ERAs. Hanuman ll, Romulus and Remus at Oulton Park.

Roger Richmond's Rolls-Royce with Hanuman II on the trailer. On one occasion the wooden box rear was filled with an agricultural substance which caused much offence when the Rolls was taken to an R-R concours gathering. Roger and Bill were in the beer tent and resisted the tannoyed appeals to move the offending vehicle. When they eventually returned, they found it in solitary splendour.

Another Rolls for Hanuman, albeit a little more modern than Roger Richmond's. This belonged to Allan Bramwell, Bill's sponsor, and was frequently used by him to get up dry river beds in order to go fishing in New Zealand's South Island.

Two Mercedes 408 diesels did sterling service over many years. They were adapted to carry the ERAs and all spares, tools as well as much domestic equipment. The one parked against the fence (in front of Romulus) carries the White Mouse symbol on its rear doors.

Bill's bachelor habit of sleeping and cooking in the van, when away racing, came to an abrupt end when Victoria joined the racing ménage; hotels and B&Bs then became the preferred habitat. Possibly due to the pre-war camp beds and the snoring of team members camping in the vicinity of the van, coupled with the distance to get to the facilities across sodden grassy paddocks in the dark and pouring rain... After racing finished for the day beer and barbecues were still as popular though, weather permitting.

Last of the line: A mini-articulated lorry which was used to bring R12C to Cadwell in 1999 and included a room for Victoria and friends!

8/10/88

Dear Duncan,

Thank you for your letter

So pleased to hear you are in contact with Paul Emery, please give him my very best regards if you see him again. He was truly an inspiration to a lot of us youngsters in the 60s although most of us could see, even in those days, that he was doomed to failure in many of the things he was undertaking. However, he was always full of help and advise, bright ideas fell out all over the place especially in the pub behind the dreadful works at Aspenlea Rd, Fulham. I still use the quick lift jack that he and I made for the E.R.A. although he put me in Paddington Hospital for 48 hrs with 'Arc-Eye' and told me it was my fault for watching what he was doing – I don't think he had a spare welding visor!! When I think of some of the things we drove on the road from that garage – we should have all been locked up, especially the twin Mini and the Omille Imp which I once raced at Brands. One of the best journeys I had with him was when Sandy Skinner was PR for Chrysler and brought round one of those Studebaker Torado things – FWD and funny Duplex chain drive from this huge V8 to the gearbox – I think it was an Auto. Paul took us all out to see if it behaved like a Mini – it didn't! I particularly remember the racing start in Hyde Park underpass which we shot out of like a champagne cork followed by a huge cloud of rubber and petrol smoke and shouts of mirth.

No I didn't know he had used the box – he never told me

It is quite safe, can you think of anybody who would have a use for it or a museum that would display it rather than stick it in a dungeon.

If your up this way – always a spare bed, good pubs and beer and plenty of real enthusiasts in the district.

Regards,
Bill

A typical letter of Bill's: in this case sent to Duncan Rabagliati about a gearbox, originally developed by Connaught, which Bill had acquired. Paul Emery had used the box on a couple of occasions and Emery's name led Bill into some vivid memories of various experiences in Emery's company many years before.

VSCC: 'Ace whinger, keen member and supporter'

Bill joined the VSCC as a young man and remained a member to the end of his life. As we have seen, its racing programme provided the framework for most of his ERA activity. Consequently, the Club's policies were important and Bill had clear views about many of them. While it might be an exaggeration to say that so did all his fellow members, the VSCC has always embraced a wide range of opinions, many strongly held and forcibly expressed.

These views emerge in different ways: one is by serving on the Club's committee which Bill did in the early 1970s. Another is through the correspondence pages of the *VSCC's Bulletin* and letters from Bill appeared here from time to time; we have already noted his readiness to 'write to the Editor' when robustly defending the re-emergence of Romulus and again in opposing the introduction of roll-over bars. Editors are sometimes written to in a private capacity and Bill was corresponding with *VSCC Bulletin* editors in this way during the 1980s and 1990s, as well as occasionally sending a 'round robin' to the Club Committee or a letter to its President when exercised on a particular issue.

One important example was eligibility. As we've suggested in Chapter Four, this is an integral part of historic racing and unlike the Hundred Years War, which did eventually cease, never capable of final settlement. It seems to be a case of temporary cease-fires until the issue flairs up again as it did in the 1980s and 1990s.

Bill knew as well as anyone that by racing historic cars, most of their parts would eventually break or wear out and therefore need replacing. Such replacements would often be newly-manufactured and eventually, as he said, "a well-used car would be 90% replica". He was therefore relatively relaxed on the issue of 'replicas', a matter that did worry many others, *providing* that they kept faith with the original design and did not avail themselves of modern technology.

It was the use of this modern technology on various 'specials' that he didn't like: "it's the 1990 specials that are spoiling it for me. They don't cost very much to build and maintain, they use enormous numbers of modern parts, quite often hidden inside original cases, use a great deal of modern technology and don't appear to be anything like the period special from the era they are supposed to come" (letter, 1997). Bill said that he and Duncan Ricketts were in no doubt that by following the same kind of recipe, they could construct a Riley 'special' which would defeat the majority of ERAs. Bill acknowledged that most of these 'specials' were skilfully constructed by excellent engineers and invariably well driven but if standard cars were obliged to race against them the

An ERA man drives other cars: while the great majority of Bill's racing was with ERAs he did sample a considerable number of other makes including some very significant historical cars. Here is a selection, (clockwise from top left):

A Royal Enfield quad bike for a Brighton run in the late 1960s. It was borrowed from Michael Ware who had gone to the Montagu/National Motor Museum at Beaulieu as Curator, then Director. Bill was accompanied by David Kergon's brother, Geoffrey and Geoffrey's wife, Mary.

Bill at the wheel of a 1922 ex-Count Zborowski, 2-litre straight-eight Miller owned by Eckart Berg, at Silverstone in June 1993 where he finished fifth.

Bill is out in John Ould's Austin 750 at Cadwell Park in 1981 where he finished second in an Austin 7 Race. He had met John when he was in Australia in 1978. John was part of the Thailand trip and raced his BMW 328 there.

Bill in action at Mallory Park in 1993. driving Eckart Berg's Delage which combines one of the chassis commissioned by Prince Chula in the 1930s and a 1927 Delage 1500cc straight-eight cylinder engine. Bill enjoyed driving this car around the Cotswold lanes and was easily enticed to his surprise 50th birthday party with the promise of a drive.

Bill powering to victory in a 5-lap handicap race at Silverstone in April 1974.

The VSCC race report states "... Peter Mann's 1924 Sunbeam (which motors faster than its appearance might suggest) started the race 1 min 40 secs ahead of Limit Man Bill Morris (driving Steven Stephenson's Frazer Nash with a BMW engine) and Bill had only just left the starting line when Mark Joseland (also in a Nash) appeared at the head of the field ... Bill Morris had worked his way up to 19th place on lap 2 and into 10th place on lap 3. Sensation at the end of the fourth lap when Battling Bill flashed by in 3rd place behind Clifford's Riley and Mark Joseland and by the end of the race he was in first place – recording, on the way, an incredible fastest lap time of 1 min 13 secs."

A most appropriate car for an ERA man – the White Riley that led directly to ERA. Bill drove it at Loton Park in 1993 when it was owned by Macko Laqueur.

inevitable result was that the latter would be driven out, sooner or later.

Bill thought these 'specials' were one important reason for the drop in entries for certain races in the 1990s: "Where have all the ERAs gone? I keep getting asked. Where have all the many other cars gone? I reply" (letter, 1997). Apart from the deterrent effect of 'specials', Bill thought there were a number of other problems which had contributed to the fall-off. The need for silencers at hill climbs and sprints was one – it was "virtually impossible to silence a highly supercharged pre-war car without risking serious engine maladies, as well as making the cars very unsightly". The VSCC was also facing increased competition and some of these alternative clubs or venues were providing benefits in cash or kind. The VSCC itself had provided some modest payment – for certain entries – up to the late 1980s but then withdrawn the scheme, which in Bill's view was "a serious mistake which had essentially started the exodus".

Bill was a 'constructive' critic so that the 'ace whinger' (his own self-description) usually had plenty of ideas about how things could be put right. As one of the VSCC's leading competitors, his views obviously carried some weight. But, as noted above, the VSCC is a club with many different interests and 'voices' and at least in the short term its approach did not move in Bill's direction. But if he felt strongly on an issue then he was going to say what he felt: "I have always been taught to scrap for what I believe in... " (letter; 1981). He knew that others would disagree but believed these differences should be frankly expressed and argued out, accepting that the eventual outcome would often be a compromise. What he particularly disliked was 'tittle-tattle and innuendo', some of which he had picked up on following his mid-1980s' rebuild of R12B. One VSCC member had phoned him up and said he understood Bill had incorporated titanium cross members. Bill thanked him for being direct and invited him to inspect the car: "if he found ANY titanium in it I would give him £1000. I also offered to provide the magnet. Alas he didn't come" (letter, 1988).

Quite apart from the substance of whatever he was arguing, Bill thought a 'scrap' had a positive value in itself: in the late 1980s after complaining to David Thirlby about one of his *Bulletin* editorials, he concluded: "Nothing like a good controversial *Bulletin* for keeping the adrenalin flowing. Keep up the good work" (letter, 1988). Bill's letters were for many years hand-written: his small neat script swept across A4 pages of blank paper filling every inch and one can catch the sense of his own 'adrenalin flowing' without much difficulty.

Amidst this talk of 'scrapping' it's important to remember the other part of Bill's self-portraiture – 'keen member and supporter'. In the 1970s, in addition to letters to the editor, he also contributed event

In the days before Health and Safety Legislation, one could do this sort of carefree activity! This is the Ford F100 transporter being used as a grass track device, laden with helpers and friends, taken at a country fair organised by Nigel Arnold Foster at Lydiard Millicent near his house close to Wootton Bassett. No prizes were awarded but a safe and good time was enjoyed by all concerned!

reports and feature articles on ERA to the *VSCC Bulletin*. After he had given up driving both he and Victoria regularly formed part of the VSCC's large body of voluntary officials indispensable to the running of its events.

Encouraging the next generation

When Bill started with R12B he was only twenty and as Chapter Two has related neither he nor David Kergon knew much about the history or the mechanics of ERAs. They learnt pretty quickly on both counts partly through hard practical experience and partly through learning from others. As we have said earlier a shared 'culture' is important in keeping cars such as ERAs active and competitive and the 'bearers' of this culture are the successive generations of owners, drivers and engineers.

As the life cycle develops the 'apprentices' in turn become the 'masters' and Bill passed on his knowledge and experience to many others. Among those who benefitted particularly from this process were Tony Stephens, John Ure and Duncan Ricketts. Tony and John both started off as helpers and then 'graduated' to racing ERAs themselves. After Tony had completed R12C's reconstruction, he raced the car for fourteen years and then had a further four seasons with Hanuman II. John Ure was a fettler for much of the 1980s before making his debut as a driver with Hanuman II. The experience he accumulated

155

BIRTHDAY PARTY

The WRGM Jubilee Bash Committee

*I*nvites you to attend his surprise birthday party on
Saturday 18 July 1992
beginning at **17.00** hours.

The chosen venue, courtesy of Julian Mazjub, Esq., is:
**Manor Farm, Little Wolford*,
Near Shipston on Stour,
Warks., CV36 5LZ.**

Dress: Imaginative/Appropriate
Enquiries: John Ure   **(0449) 676006**
 or Victoria Read   **(0908) 674064**

*West of A34 between Chipping Norton and Shipston on Stour

The invitation to the celebration of Bill's 50th birthday.

All the preparations were made without his knowledge so he arrived at Julian Mazjub's home entirely unsuspecting in Eckart's Delage, to find over 100 friends and family assembled with a mouthwatering array of machinery.

His favourite meal – sheep, peas and tatties, had been translated into spitroast lamb, petit pois and buttered new potatoes, along with a magnificent buffet of other culinary delights, plenty of Pimms, wines and his favourite local beer on tap – 'Hookie' Hook Norton.

A top Jazz band played and the party stretched long into the night. Bill enjoyed himself so much he couldn't remember anything after 10pm, luckily, photographs reminded him later.

Another surprise was this full size preselector gearbox birthday cake, which he cut with a hacksaw!

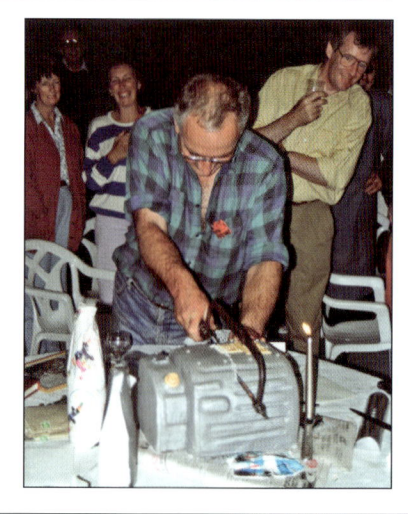

An unsuspecting Bill arrives with Christa Berg beside him

A few of the assembled modes of transport

The birthday 'present': The parachute that 'wrapped' it was pulled off to reveal this hilarious assemblage of his two least favourite vehicles, then the door to the caravan fell open and three Australian friends fell out, well oiled with Aussie red to surprise him further!

His dislike of Reliant Robins related to early days of self employment, when he agreed to do a small job on a local elderly lady's Robin. Having completed the work, he put the car into reverse to back out of the workshop, forgetting he had not replaced the boards over the pit so the nose fell into the void leaving him trapped in the car with both doors jammed shut! He managed to escape through the back door and winched it up enough to insert the boards. Having explained the creased doors to the owner he asked her never to bring it through his gate again.

A bemused Bill!

Sid Day, Gordon Chapman, Bruce Spollon, Victoria Morris and Rodney Felton

157

with Bill, both on the mechanical side and at the wheel, was put to good use on other ERAs he drove – often with great success – as well as in preparing cars for other owners. Although Duncan Ricketts had acquired the skills of car body-making before he met Bill the latter played an important role in enabling him to specialise in work on racing cars; additionally it was Bill's recommendation that Duncan should be responsible for both the preparation and driving of R1B, following Patrick Marsh's premature death. Since Duncan began with R1B in 1987 he has built up a fine reputation both as a driver and as a preparer, embracing a wide range of ERAs. Of course Tony, John and Duncan are all highly skilled and able individuals and very much their own men but all would acknowledge the importance of the initial opportunity Bill gave them.

Another significant flow of 'apprentices' came from Bill's Australian connections which, as we have seen, were first established in the late 1970s. Greg Snape is a notable example: Bill met Greg's father, Graeme, during his first expedition to Australia and that led in due course to Greg coming over to work for Bill on the gearboxes. Subsequently Greg drove R12C both in the U.K. and Australia and played a very important role in the recreation – and driving – of the Kiefts. Greg was far from the only 'Aussie' to pick up vital skills at Leafield. He had been preceded by at least fifteen other youngsters many of whom, after working for Bill, moved on to more 'modern' forms of racing including Formula One Grand Prix teams.

Quite apart from these particular examples of Bill's influence, his forty years in historic racing brought him into contact with a very large number of people. Bill was always most willing to pass on his accumulated experience and, in turn, he learnt much from his wide range of friendship and acquaintance. Many of the latter came together in July 1992 at the invitation of the 'WRGM Jubilee Bash Committee' to celebrate Bill's 50th birthday. It was held at Julian Mazjub's home in the Cotswolds and in addition to the usual food and drink a number of well-known racing and sports cars were present to join in the celebrations. A special cake had been commissioned in the form of a preselector gearbox complete with edible oily rag and spanner; Bill cut the cake with a hacksaw! The Committee had also assembled a mock White Mouse Equipe consisting of an old caravan and a Reliant Robin – both at the bottom of Bill's list of desirable wheeled vehicles. Bill was invited to wreak destruction on this ensemble demonstrating that even for someone whose overwhelming concern was conservation and preservation there were limits!

Conclusion

In 1971 Bill said "I first saw an ERA when I was 12 and to me at that early age the ERA was the epitome of what a racing car should be: functional, fun to watch and very noisy. Over the last seventeen years I would only change this view a little and say, functional, fun to drive and very noisy". Bill's involvement with ERAs continued more or less for the rest of his life, even after the sale of R12C in 2006-7. He remained closely in touch with what was happening to ERAs and, more generally, to historic racing.

These chapters have therefore told the story of an ERA man – ERA being at the centre of Bill's motor racing for much longer than any other car. Such a focus acknowledges that Bill drove other racing and sports cars and, in the final years of his life, devoted much time and energy to reconstructing the GP V8 'Godiva' 2.5 litre Coventry Climax Kieft and the V8 4.5 litre De Soto Kieft sports car. It was also true that Bill had plenty of 'hinterland' – a variety of interests outside motor sport which

The two Kiefts, together at Leafield in 2009

Bill's vision and expertise in completing these big Kiefts and introducing them to international racing, may be seen as potentially more significant than his contribution to the ERA marque. In particular, the single seater poses an intriguing 'what if' question when viewed in the context of British racing history.

Two wheels as well as four: Bill and Victoria were strong enthusiasts for travel on two wheels and here they are setting out for a spin into the Oxfordshire countryside. Bill is on the only black MV Agusta 750S the factory made and Victoria on her Benelli 254 Quattro.

embraced parish council work, music and theatre, ornithology and environmental projects. So, while Bill's life was in no sense just an ERA one, ERA was the dominant strand.

Much as Bill admired ERAs as a teenager the key step on the ERA road was the decision, made jointly with David Kergon, to buy R12B in 1962. Once it arrived back in the U.K. from Rhodesia admiration from a distance was exchanged for the decidedly hands-on experience of actually owning, preparing, and racing an ERA. As these chapters have recounted Bill's involvement in ERA matters progressively deepened with the major overhaul of R12B in 1965/6 followed by the subsequent rebuilds in the mid-1980s and early 1990s. The collection and assembling of parts for the reconstruction of R12C involved both familiar problems and many new dilemmas. Similarly responsibility for the overhaul, and then the driving, of Romulus were demanding tasks with a car so rich in historical associations. Driving the E type GP2 for Gordon Chapman was demanding in another way – an involvement with a model that both the works and private owners had found unpredictable and which had provoked many questions but with few clear answers.

Buying R12B in 1962 and joining the 'ERA gang' meant that Bill and David were part of a group of owner-drivers who in nearly every case also prepared their cars. This was the predominant pattern in the 1960s and 1970s and indeed into the 1980s when historic racing for cars of the 1930s reached its high point. Since then the scene has clearly shifted – sadly, though to some extent inevitably, the generation who took on ERAs in the late 1950s or early 1960s have died or retired and a new one has come forward. There is now more division between owners, drivers and preparers, the structure of historic racing has shifted with new promoters and additional venues and ERAs, though still attracting considerable interest, are only one group in a constantly expanding constituency of 'historic' racing which on occasion subsumes cars of the 1970s or even 1980s.

Dougal Marr who himself raced with one of the formidable 1935/6 V8–RI Maseratis knew Bill and the other leading participants in 1970s and 1980s historic racing and some years later powerfully evoked the atmosphere they generated, so let's leave the last word to him:

"I watched Bill (Morris), Hamish (Moffatt), Tony (Stephens), David Black, Rodney Felton, Patrick Marsh, Martin Morris and a host of other characters working furiously in the pits at each meeting to ensure they were ready for the race to come. Indeed some heroic rebuilds took place in the Paddock as parts gave way under the stress of qualifying. But these meetings were for enthusiasts, cars had to be right, the paddock was 'where it was at' and in those days we could all hang over the pit wall to watch. The cognoscenti would come and have informed debates round the cars though this became a lot more informal as the afternoon wore on and the beer tent came into play. What impressed me most though was the enthusiasm for getting out on to the track. It was just like the crew of a fighter squadron. The banter and joie de vivre were hiding the preparation and steely resolve.

With the racing programme underway we all crammed round the pit wall to watch the cars as they hurtled past. As the day wore on cars seemed to be arriving over the finish line more and more sideways and battles became extremely exciting. In the heat of the action the concern for the longevity of carefully prepared machinery seemed to go by the board as the red mist arrived. Some races were memorable because of the closeness of the finish, others because of a battling challenge from the back of the field. Sometimes it was just two or three cars changing the lead throughout the race... While Maseratis, Alfas and Bugattis were always in the fray it was often the close racing between the ERAs that caught the attention.

Bill, Hamish, Patrick, Tony and others had completed remarkable restorations of their respective cars and were out to show us what real racing had been about in the pre- and early post-war era. The cars were immaculate, Bill's R12B looking as though Bira had only just got out of it, Hamish's R3A in a piece of one-upmanship with all body panel screws lovingly wire locked. The engines then were remarkably close to original with the two-litre cars having an edge over the one-and-a-halfs. Hamish and Bill were often in close company and, on one particular day at Silverstone, were battling it out to the finish. Both came into the pits, flushed with exertion and being humorously abusive. Having suffered at Bill's hands on the circuit Hamish sounded off "Bill is quite mad! No. Very brave! The reason is that he's quite blind, which explains his late braking since he clearly doesn't realise that a corner is coming up until he has arrived in the middle of it!" Hoots of laughter all round with cries of pot-calling-kettle-black! The fact was that the standard of driving in this vintage environment was extremely high with only a few exceptions. There were no heated verbals in the paddock, the cars were driven to their limits on occasions but not at the expense of others and that's what made our meetings so very different."

Footnote

Bill died on May 5th 2009 at home, after a long illness that did not dampen his enthusiasm for living life to the full or curb his spirit in any way. His friends and family gave him the support and encouragement to do this. He was laid to rest after spending two days in his garage between his GP Kieft and MV Agusta, in a wicker casket suitably embellished with racing mementoes and roses. Ben and Victoria delivered him to the Leafield Natural Burial Ground on a hilltop a mile from the village at a speed he would have thoroughly approved of – a fitting finale for a racing man.

ERA and driver at rest.

Index

Ackerman; 105
Acton; 87
Africa; 33, 34, 35, 59, 87
A.I.A.C.R; 18
AJM-1 see ERA;
Albi; 133
Alfa Romeo; 49, 51, 63, 72, 76, 77, 105, 126, 161
Allan, Gordon; 46
Allcomers' Race; 63, 120, 121, 140
Alta; 146
Amilcar; 126
Armco; 56, 126
Armstrong; 59
Armstrong-Siddeley; 60, 146
Arnold Foster, Nigel; 155
Ashmore, J; 24
Aston Martin; 29, 33, 36, 40, 42, 81, 89, 92, 125
Austin; 29, 30, 36, 65, 152
Australia; 60, 61, 63, 64, 67, 80, 99, 108, 109, 152, 157, 158
Australian GP; 64, 65, 66, 108, 125
Australian Jubilee Scratch Race; 65
Australian PM; 66
Autokits; 39
Autospeed Garage; 26, 28
Autosport; 63
Aviation Blue; 101

Bangkok Grand Prix; 69, 72, 75, 128
Bangkok; 69, 70, 72, 73, 77

Barker, Harold; 97
Barker, Harold; 97
Bass Straights; 109
Battersea; 34
Beaulieu; 111, 115, 131, 152
Becketts; 122
Benelli; 107, 160
Bentley; 49, 146
Bentley-Napier; 128
Berg, Christa; 156
Berg, Eckart; 152, 156
Berry, Jim; 84, 85, 88, 89, 133, 134
Berry, Vera; 84, 85
Berthon, Peter; 13, 16
Bira; see Birabongse
Birabongse HRH Prince; 17, 18, 19, 20, 23, 24, 43, 60, 69, 74, 76, 84, 85, 101, 111, 112, 119, 126, 129, 130, 131
Bishop's Bridge Road; 35
Black, David; 64, 161
BMW; 72, 152, 153
Bob Gerard Trophy; 77, 79
Bodmin; 85
Body, Bill; 122, 130, 131
Bolster, John; 49
Bond, Michael; 33, 34
Border Reivers; 25, 27
Bourne; 13, 40, 107, 108
Boysy; see Clube
Brady, P; 72
Bramwell, Allan; 67, 69, 148
Bramwell, Sue; 69
Brands Hatch; 36, 37, 43, 91
Brettell, Terence; 120, 137, 138
Brewer, Peter; 53, 84, 85, 111

British Embassy; 72
British Grand Prix; 124, 142
British Leyland; 90, 91
British Week; 42
BRM; 107, 108, 125, 137,
Bronson, Julian; 104
Brooklands; 14, 20, 80, 85, 100, 122
Brown, Bertie; 111
Brown, David; 92
BRSCC; 53
Bugatti Owners' Club; 51
Bugatti Trust; 141
Bugatti; 49, 50, 63, 65, 66, 72, 126, 133, 161
Bulawayo; 33
Burford; 95
Burton, George; 49

Cadwell; 40, 55, 58, 76, 108, 122, 125, 137, 138, 139, 140, 149, 152
Case; 69
Chakrabongse House; 73
Chakrabongse, HRH Prince Chula; 17, 22, 23, 24, 74, 76, 80, 84, 85, 94, 101, 110, 112, 113, 115, 119, 122, 131, 152
Chakrabongse, HRH Princess Chula; 52, 85, 86, 88, 89, 92, 94, 111, 112, 115, 130, 131
Chakrabongse, MR Narisa; 17, 58, 60, 69, 72, 74, 75, 76, 77, 94, 114, 115, 122, 124, 125, 128, 129, 130, 131

164

Chapman, Gordon; 89, 134, 135, 136, 138, 141, 142, 143, 157, 160
Chapman, Jeannie; 143
Chapman, Lucy; 141, 142, 143
Chapman, Narisa; 141, 142, 143
Charterhall; 20
Chavalit Yongcharyudh; 71
Chelsea; 34
Chevrolet; 33
Chrysler; 55
Chula, see Chakrabongse
Clark, James; 69
Classic, Brian; 63, 128
Clay Hill; 138
Clifford; 153
Clube, Malcolm; 36
Concours d'etat; 45
Connaught; 124, 146, 147, 150
Cook, Humphrey; 13, 29, 133
Cooper Bristol; 26, 68, 69, 122
Cooper; 67, 68
Cooper-ERA; 88
Copse; 61
Cork; 18
Corner, Neil; 51, 53, 59, 126
Cornwall; 52
Cotswolds; 152, 158
Country Gentleman Racing & Sports Car Club; 67
Coventry Climax; 159
Coys; 55, 105
Crabb, Terry; 109
Crash; 21
Cricklewood; 31
Crosthwaite, R; 88
Crystal Palace; 16, 43, 54
Cumbria; 89
Curragh; 106, 108

Daily Express; 44
Day, Donald; 40, 94, 128
Day, Sid; 40, 157

de Cadenet, Alain; 76
De Ram; 23, 24, 59, 117, 123
De Soto; 159
Delage; 17, 49, 152, 156
Delahaye; 49
Dobson, Arthur; 15, 20
Dominion Blue; 101
Donington Museum; 143
Donington; 19, 40, 55, 58, 63, 70, 76, 80, 82, 98, 99, 104, 105, 109, 128, 135, 137, 138
Drummond, Vic; 28
Dunedin; 68, 69
Dunlop; 65
Durban; 111
Dusseldorf; 42

Ebblewhite, A V; 85
Ecurie Ecosse; 26
Edwards, Verdun; 26, 133
Elmgren, Gunnar; 123
Emery, Paul; 150
England, F R W ("Lofty"); 18
ENV; 146
ERA -
  R12B; 13 onwards
  R12C; 13 onwards
  R12B/C; 23
  Hanuman; 18 onwards
  Hanuman II; 23 onwards
  Remus; 18 onwards
  Romulus; 18 onwards
  Chassis numbers:
    R1A; 46, 142
    R2A; 134
    R3A; 111, 161
    R4A; 28, 33, 52, 98, 99
    R1B; 78, 80, 91, 158
    R2B; 18 onwards
    R4C; 15
    R4D; 17, 19, 53, 63, 79, 84, 85, 88, 92, 98, 99
    R5B; 18 onwards
    R8B; 23, 80
    R8C; 89
    R10B; 65
    R11B; 89, 125, 126

    R14B; 128
    GP1; 20 onwards
    GP2; 26 onwards
    AJM-1; 138
    ERA Delage; 59, 72
    ERA Jaguar; 133
    ERA Special; 133
ERA Club; 40, 77
Eton; 49
Europe; 34, 50, 55

Fairfield, Pat; 15, 16
Felton, Rodney; 64, 74, 76, 157, 161
Ferarri; 49, 68
Festival of Speed; 55
Finlayson, Jock; 36
Finn, Joel; 65
Fitzgerald, Jim; 93
Fitzpatrick, J; 72
Flint, Ken; 26, 133
Ford F100; 37, 50, 148, 155
Ford GT40; 34
Ford Special; 65
Formula I; 56
Fraser, Malcolm; 66
Fraser-Nash; 30, 153
Freeman, John; 42
Fry, Joe; 33

G K N; 95
G N; 36
Gahagan, Dudley; 41, 111
Geelong; 67
Gerard, Bob; 28, 85, 88, 94
Germany; 42, 107
Giddings, P; 72
Gillespie, Alan; 28, 32, 33, 34
Gloucestershire; 141
Goddard, David; 30
Goddard, Geoff; 30
Goddard, John; 65
Godfrey, George; 90, 93, 94, 98, 102, 140
Gold Leaf Trophy; 63
Goodwood Revival; 55, 143
Goodwood; 25, 26, 55, 61, 63
Gothenburg; 49, 50

165

Green Man; 128
Green Willie; 128
Gresham's School; 29
Gurston; 31

H W M; 146, 147
Haddenham; 91
Hall, Brian; 88
Hammersmith; 18, 103
Hampshire, David; 24, 39
Hannen, Peter; 64
Hanuman II, see E R A
Hanuman, see E R A
Harlesden; 34, 35
Harper, John; 79
Harrison, Cuth; 89
Hartford; 59, 60, 104
Hawkins, Paul; 34, 49
Hawthorne Memorial Trophy; 98, 122
Hawthorne Spanish Trophy; 105, 138, 140
Hawthorne, Mike; 43
Hay, Neville; 107
Head, Patrick; 125
Heath Robinson; 101
Hill, Phil; 80, 81
Historic G P Cars Association; 55
Holgate, Stanley; 22, 32, 39, 85, 88
Holt, Norfolk; 30
Horsfall; 42
Howe, Earl; 23, 80
Hull, Douglas; 41, 48, 50
Hull; 49, 88

Invicta; 136
Ireland; 20, 106, 123
Irish Sea; 108
Isle of Man; 133
J B W – Maserati; 84
J C B Championship; 55
Jaguar; 33, 50, 107, 133, 134
James Clark Memorial Trophy; 69
Jamieson, Tom Murray; 13, 25, 39, 102

Jarvies, Alistair; 70
Jenkinson, Denis; 48, 87, 124, 129, 131
Jordan, Brian; 39, 94
Joseland, Mark; 153

Karslkoga, Sweden; 48, 50
Kergon, David; 29 onwards
Kergon, Geoffrey; 45, 49, 152
Kergon, Mary; 152
Kieft; 125, 143, 158, 159, 163
Kimber, Lawrie; 90

Lagonda; 146
Lancaster Gate Mews; 35, 36, 39, 85, 94, 145
Landrover; 92, 145
Lane, M;
Laqueur, Macko; 153
Laystalls; 22
Le Mans; 34
Leafield; 37, 58, 59, 64, 88, 94, 95, 96, 102, 114, 115, 117, 125, 145, 158, 159, 163
Lehoux, Marcel; 22
Leicester; 85
Leston, Les; 46
Lindsay, Hon Patrick; 40, 41, 42, 49, 50, 62, 63, 64, 75, 96, 111, 121, 122, 126, 128
Lindsay, Ludovic; 62, 63, 64, 72, 74, 77
Linger, Barry; 95, 103, 105
Little Budworth; 62
Little Rissington; 95
Liverpool; 26, 133
Lloyds & Scottish; 55
Lockhart, Frank; 122
Lodge Plugs; 130
London Evening News; 120
London Toy & Model Museum; 128
Loton Park; 55, 82, 153
Lotus; 32, 33, 34
Lower End; 145
Lucas, Charles; 36
Lydiard, Millicent; 155

M G; 28, 63, 65, 72, 77, 91, 146
M V Agusta; 36, 160, 163
Macclesfield; 85
Maggots; 93
Mallala; 108
Mallory Park; 55, 79, 101, 105, 152
Mann, Peter; 153
Marr, Doug; 160
Marsh, Patrick; 41, 78, 90, 128, 158, 161
Marsh, Sally; 78, 90
Martin Ford; 33
Maserati; 63, 64, 65, 68, 72, 74, 76, 78, 82, 125, 126, 142, 146, 10, 161
Massey, Peter; 111
May, Tim; 8, 107
Mayman, Anthony; 63, 72, 93, 94
Mayman, Chris; 138
Mays, Raymond; 13, 14, 29, 33, 84, 85, 107, 108, 109
Mazjub, Julian; 103, 156, 158
McCrossan, Oliver; 106
McDonald, Jim; 64, 65, 66
Mercedes; 126, 149
Merrick, Tony; 46
Millar, Cameron; 78
Miller; 152
Moffat, Hamish; 49, 50, 161
Molina, Lou; 65, 72, 73
Monaco; 63, 78, 81, 125, 126, 127, 128
Montagu Motor Museum; 111, 113, 115
Montagu, Lord; 130
Montien Hotels; 71
Morris, Ben; 60, 73, 75, 79, 80, 97, 98, 123, 129, 163
Morris, Bill; 29 onwards
Morris, Martin; 41, 42, 58, 60, 121, 125, 126, 128, 161
Morris, Victoria (sister); 29, 30, 32, 34
Morris, Victoria; 58, 75, 101, 106, 108, 149, 155, 157, 160, 163

Moss, Bill; 30
Motor Sport; 28, 29, 48, 56, 76, 78, 83, 120, 122, 129, 130, 131
Motoring News; 123
Murray Jamieson; see Jamieson
Murray, David; 24, 39
Murray, Sandy; 40, 85

National Motor Museum; 129, 152
Narisa, see Chakrabongse
New Zealand; 67, 69, 78, 84, 135, 148
Nurburgring; 55
Nockolds, Roy; 47
Norton, Tom; 84
Nicholson, John; 133, 134
Nuffield Trophy; 19, 20, 58, 63, 105
Nuneaton; 60
Nye, Doug; 133

Orchard; 141
Ould, John; 72, 152
Oulton Park; 8, 40 45, 48, 62, 76, 81, 84, 98, 104, 105, 121, 122, 130, 135, 136, 137, 138, 139, 140, 148
Owen, Denys; 26
Oxfordshire; 145, 160

Paris; 49
Parnell, Reg; 24
Patrick Lindsay Trophy Race; 59, 79
Pattaya; 74, 75, 76
Paul Ricard; 58
Philip Island; 64, 108, 109
Phillips, Simon; 122
Phoenix Park; 63, 109, 122, 123
Pichon, J; 49
Pirelli; 65
Porsche; 15, 16, 19, 98
Porton, Wilts; 31
Potts, R W; 88
Prescott; 40, 47, 51, 57, 58, 82, 140, 141

Pre-War Allcomers Race; 121, 122, 137

Queens Gate Mews; 35

R A C.M S A; 56
R.12.B; see E R A
R.12.C; see E R A
R.12B/C; see E R A
Rabagliati, Duncan; 150
Rahm, Shura; 85
Rajdamnern Avenue; 72, 73, 76
Ramayana; 18
Ramponi, G; 36
Read, Victoria; 58 (see also Morris, Victoria)
Reims; 20, 21, 22, 80, 85
Reliant Robin; 157, 158
Remus; see E R A
Rhodesia, Southern; 26, 35, 80, 160
Richmond, Roger; 115, 122, 127, 128, 129, 130, 148
Ricketts, Duncan; 58, 67, 78, 79, 80, 90, 91, 109, 134, 142, 143, 151, 155, 158
Ricketts, James; 143
Riley; 30, 31, 33, 42, 65, 104, 146, 147, 151, 153
Rivers Fletcher; 40, 51, 100
Road and Track; 80
Rockell, Billy; 36
Rolls Royce; 49, 148
Romulus; see E R A
Rose, Harry; 48
Rouen; 48, 49
Rover; 122
Royal Enfield; 152
Royal New Zealand Air Force; 68
Royer-Collard, Peter; 36, 38, 46, 51, 101
Rubery Owen; 87
Rush, Peter; 38, 51
Russia; 68
Ruston Mews; 36

S U Carburettors; 135

Salisbury, Southern Rhodesia; 27, 32, 33
Sanskrit; 18
Sarnpasiri Viriyasiri; 71
Saunders, Dr Stuart; 65, 66, 72
Saunders; 66
Scott; 30
Seaman Trophy Race; 45, 46, 47, 48, 62, 105, 121, 124, 128, 135, 138, 139, 140
Seaman, Richard; 17, 36, 40
Self Changing Gears; 146
Seven Seas Fellowship Challenge Trophy; 54
Shearer, Kevin; 65, 66
Shell Thailand; 71
Shelsley Walsh; 14, 33, 40, 55, 58, 100
Sheppard, Geoff; 139
Shuttleworth; 63
Siam; see Thailand
Silverstone; 31, 40, 42, 44, 46, 48, 55, 58, 61, 62, 63, 64, 80, 96, 97, 98, 99, 101, 105, 117, 118, 119, 120, 121, 122, 124, 125, 128, 129, 134, 138, 142, 143, 152, 153
Singha Beer; 71
Skinner, Sandy; 36, 47
Smith, Norman; 133
Smith, W H; 146
Smiths Industries; 29, 30, 31, 38, 51, 94, 111, 115, 145
Snape, Graeme; 159
Snape, Greg; 108, 109, 158
Snetterton; 29, 38, 44
Somervail, Jim; 25, 26, 28
South Africa; 26, 27, 44, 94, 115
Spain; 107
Spollon, Bruce; 157
Sporting Motorist; 39
Sprinzel, John; 36, 37, 50
Squire; 146
Stephens, A K (Tony); 72, 76, 77, 78, 79, 80, 82, 90, 91, 94, 95, 96, 98, 100, 103, 105, 129, 155, 158, 161
Stephenson, Steven; 153

Stow on the Wold; 95
Straight, Whitney; 36
Suez Canal; 34
Suffolk; 56
Summers, Bill; 49
Sunbeam; 49, 153
Sweden; 48, 49, 50
Sweet, Roger; 72, 73, 74, 77
Sydney Marathon; 49

Talbot; 126, 146
Thai International; 71
Thailand; 17, 18, 22, 44, 61, 63, 69, 70, 71, 73, 74, 75, 76, 77, 114, 126, 128, 129, 152
The Times; 36
Thirlby, David; 154
Tilbury; 34
Timaru; 69
Tingle, Sam; 26, 27, 28
Tredethy; 52, 85, 88
Tring; 86
Turnberry; 26
Turnell, Cyril; 60, 145, 146

Ulster Trophy; 23, 24
Ulysse Nardin; 85
Ure, John; 76, 80, 81, 105, 127, 135, 142, 156, 158

USA; 129

Valdez, A; 72
Venables Llewelyn, Sir John; 62, 63, 72, 74, 98, 99
Vertex; 147
Vessey, John; 89
VSCC Bulletin; 45, 47, 48, 62, 64, 66, 115, 120, 122, 128, 137, 151, 154, 155
VSCC; 26, 40, 55, 56, 58, 60, 61, 62, 63, 70, 79, 80, 89, 96, 97, 98, 99, 100, 101, 108, 119, 121, 124, 125, 134, 137, 138, 140, 151, 153, 154, 155

Wakefield Motorsport Park; 67
Walker, Peter; 133
Waller, Peter; 40, 49, 60
Walters, Bob; 43
Ware, Michael; 61, 152
Weguelin, David; 22, 91, 114, 115, 124
Wenman, David; 83
Wharton, Ken; 33, 84
Wheatcroft, Tom; 135
Whenuapai Wings and Wheels Classic Show; 68
Whenuapai; 67, 68

White Mouse Ball; 75
White Mouse Garage; 22, 38, 80 103
White Mouse; 16, 17, 24, 75, 81, 85, 127, 130, 149, 158
White Riley; 153
Whitehead, Peter; 65
Whitney; 37, 145
Whitsun Trophy; 25
Whitten, Gregory; 129
Wigram; 69
Williams & Pritchard; 89, 134
Williams F1; 125
Wills Finecast; 39
Wilson, Major W G; 145
Wiltshire; 31
Winfield; 26
Winton; 67
Wiscombe; 55, 58
Woodcote; 64, 96, 97
Wootton Bassett; 155
Wrottesley Road; 34, 35, 42

Zandvoort; 55
Zborowski, Count; 152
ZF; 25, 58
Zimbabwe; 26
Zoller; 14, 16, 23, 25, 39, 93, 94, 102, 103, 135, 139, 140